W9-CEP-817

Herbs to Grow Indoors

For Flavor, for Fragrance, for Fun

Other Works by the Author

Books
A MERRY CHRISTMAS HERBAL
HERBS IN FIVE SEASONS

Booklets
Saints in My Garden
The Book of Valentine Remembrances
Plants of Shakespeare
The Book of Thyme
Fragrances
Caprilands Grandmother's Geraniums
Herb Gardens of Delight

Herbs to Grow Indoors

For Flavor, for Fragrance, for Fun

by Adelma Grenier Simmons

Illustrated by Kathleen Bourke

A Helen Van Pelt Wilson Book

Hawthorn Books, Inc., Publishers, New York

HERBS TO GROW INDOORS

 All inquiries should be addressed to Hawthorn Books, Inc., 260 Madison Avenue, New York, New York 10016. This book was manufactured in the United States of America and published simultaneously in Canada by Prentice-Hall of Canada, Ltd., 1870 Birchmount Road, Scarborough, Ontario.

Library of Congress Catalog Card Number: 73-85441
ISBN: 0-8015-3416-X

5 6 7 8 9 10

Contents

Winter Occupation

I write about the garden,
I sing about the herbs,
I spin my yarns of leaf
    and flower
Throughout the winter days.

A.G.S.

Herbs to Grow Indoors

For Flavor, for Fragrance, for Fun

Introduction

The Alluring World of Herbs

When I write or talk about herbs, the subject closest to my life, I feel that I should begin with my own definition of them. Herbs are plants that are useful to man for flavor, for fragrance, for medicinal purposes, for magic, for charms and incantations, and for fun.

Each person limits the plants in these categories according to his own knowledge, increasing his range as his information grows. To the novice the herb world is small. The person interested primarily in health thinks of the medicinal herbs that have been recommended for generations for the treatment of various ills.

The earliest plant records emphasize herbs for healing rather than flavoring, and the roster of plants so used is enormous. Included in it are many plants that are considered purely ornamental today—the rose, hollyhock, peony, and foxglove, to mention a few of those best known. Still other herbs, now classified as vegetables, were used as medicines: carrots (still used as a curative), beets, and beans. Even stinging nettles and plantain (which is now included on herbal lists) were included.

There are many fruit trees which may be considered herbal, since from the beginning of medical research and perfume making they have been useful components of herb gardens. Thus the apple, quince, lemon, and olive are truly members of herb families and dwarf varieties can be included in indoor herb gardens. Purely fragrant plants can also be a part of this garden. Lavender, jasmine, and sweet-olive are good examples.

The garden of the gourmet is really the smallest of all, certainly for the beginner, although as his knowledge increases and his sense of adventure heightens he will find himself going beyond the important but common basic herbs—parsley, chives, thyme, rosemary—to more exotic seasonings and experimental combinations. Adventure is the keynote of herbal cookery.

Growing herbs indoors brings about an intimate relationship with these far travelers of the plant world. In your window garden you will have natives of the Orient, an abundance of Mediterranean plants and small shrubs, geraniums from South Africa, and flavoring agents from northern Scotland, the Orkney Islands, and the cold lands around the Bering Sea.

Here at Caprilands, in the cold days of winter when snow lies on the ground, green things have special significance. Now, without the distraction of a lush landscape, we are drawn closer to the intimate small plants that we choose to winter inside.

I am reminded then that the desire to bring summer indoors is as old as civilization. The effort to rescue plants from the cruel frost, to force blooms out of season, to have sweet-odored leaves close at hand, and to harbor greens for seasoning and medicinal purposes has occupied priests and monks, farmers, apothecaries, Roman senators, horticulturists, and housewives from remote pre-Christian times. The forcing of fruit branches was a ritual in central and northern Europe. This led gradually to the planting of small trees in tubs to live and bloom indoors.

Some of the landed Roman gentry, including such famous men as Cicero, Seneca, and the younger Pliny, practiced advanced forms of horticulture and wrote about their experiences in an informative and engaging manner. Their tender plants, which even the mild Italian winters destroyed, were forced by heat under thin sheets of mica, glass being then unknown, and warm water was piped around roses to coax them into bloom. The Romans were successful also in growing winter herbs and vegetables, although Seneca condemned such practices. "Live they not against nature," he wrote, "that in winter long for the rose, and by the nourishment of warm waters cause the lily, a spring flower, to bloom?"

For centuries plantsmen have argued pro and con on the subject of going against nature, but the courageous and the experimental have fought for their precious tender plants and have continued to produce June gardens in January. The gardening monks of northern Europe, who grew trees and shrubs from southern Europe in their summer gardens, found ways to house these plants during the cold season so that they could appear in their accustomed places in the spring. Potted plants, both green and flowering, played an important role in medieval gardens, both religious and secular, and among those that were highly prized were orange, lemon, fig, myrtle, bay, and the fragrant rosemary of many legends.

To the gardening monks, these plants had religious significance as well as medicinal value. They were also useful in decorating the church and altar. Laymen, through sentiment and tradition, associated them with weddings, courtship, domestic happiness, virtue, and good fortune. Thus they were important in homes.

On English estates during the eighteenth and nineteenth centuries, wintering under glass was practiced in the grand manner. Orange and other fruit trees and tender herbal shrubs from southern Europe were grown in architectural masterpieces of wood and glass called orangeries. Here fashionable people could stroll at leisure or rest on classic benches, safe from the winter chill, in a green and fragrant world.

The smaller realm of the English cottager comes closer to our country's heritage. Cottage windows were always filled with "wintered-in" plants, garnered from the dooryard garden for both protection and convenience. Inside, on stormy days, a leaf could be snipped from a favorite herb to season a meat pie or add zest to a stuffing. A cluster could scent the house.

Some of the best-liked herbs were brought by the colonists to New England and New France. The long difficult voyage and the dearth of fresh water aboard the ships made any surviving plants seem especially precious. A few hardy herbs were reputed to survive on windowsills, although they had to be carefully guarded and it must have been a major task to carry them safely into springtime.

Of this struggle with the elements, Willa Cather writes memorably in *Shadows on the Rock,* a story of early Quebec. In that bleak place, the apothecary's young daughter kept French traditions so alive that visitors to the drug shop made excuses to peer behind the medicine cupboards into the living quarters for a glimpse that reminded them of their European homeland. So successful was she in creating this illusion with her growing herbs that "Even the strange, bitter, mysterious Bishop Laval . . . asked for a sprig from a box of parsley that was growing there even in winter, and carried it away in his hand."

Often when I have stumbled half asleep through an ice-cold silent farmhouse, putting newspapers against windows etched with frost, I have thought sympathetically of all the lonely farm women who have struggled bravely to save bits of green seasoning from the cold grasp of winter.

A.G.S.

Caprilands Herb Farm
Coventry, Connecticut
March, 1969

Part One

Success with Herbs Indoors

1

Planning the Indoor Herb Garden

An indoor herb garden can be modest or pretentious depending upon your zeal and the space available. It may consist of a few plants in attractive containers or a large collection of herbs arranged on tables, shelves, and stands. A southern window is an ideal location, especially if you are interested in flowers, but many herbs will grow well in a window that provides good light but little or no sun.

The Winter Window Garden at Caprilands

At Caprilands, when Christmas is over and the long holiday season is a pleasant memory, when the guests have gone and the shop bell is silent, the quiet of winter closes around us. The Christmas greens have been taken down, cut, and scattered as a protection over perennials in the outdoor garden. Midwinter decorations have taken their place.

The living room seems large and somewhat bare without the six Christmas trees, but there are now other decorations that express the contemplative mood of this quiet season. The fire burns bright in the keeping-room fireplace. The gay reds and greens and the flashing golds of the holidays have given way to what friends call our "blue period." Draperies of handwoven fabrics that blend with the red of the walls are hardly noticed, and the old geometric hooked rugs in faded pink-reds and soft blues are back now that there are no spike heels to mutilate them. The deep blue of handwoven coverlets is repeated in Staffordshire, in pottery from Mexico's Puebla, and in a precious tea set of Italian Gubbio.

At this hour, the world outside is pink with the flush of sunset, the hills are deep blue and far away, the giant oak stretches bare arms against the sky, and beyond the sleeping garden an expanse of snow fields fringed with woods gives us a pleasant feeling of seclusion.

Stretched across the southern windows of the long room is our indoor herb garden. The draperies that almost cover the two windows from April to January are drawn far aside to admit full light. The herb collection gives the room an open, verdant look that suggests a springtime garden. A bench eight feet long and sixteen inches wide extends across the two windows. In front a lower bench of old chestnut provides a second level. Plants also occupy two side tables, and there are large pots of them on the floor. At either end are two racks and three shelves forty-five inches long and sixteen inches wide, also of old chestnut to match the long bench and the beams of the ceiling.

In this space, more than a hundred plants are growing in pots from two to twelve inches in size. The atmosphere is cool, almost cold, at night, and on windy frigid days when the temperature outside drops to zero or below, tender plants must be moved back from the windowsill. In the past, brown paper or newspaper was placed against the windows for insulation. Today, soft plastic stretched across the cold glass provides ample protection. On very cold nights, an extra sheet of plastic is draped lightly around the whole planting. This is removed as soon as the sun comes in and normal conditions prevail.

The design of the window garden is centered on a St. Francis birdbath which stands midway between the two windows on the long bench. On each side of it is a large rosemary plant in a ten-inch terracotta pot. In front of the birdbath, which I keep filled with water except on bitter nights, is a terracotta basket of tender ivies. They tumble luxuriantly over the edge. Miniature orange trees—one in full fruit and the other in bloom—flank the ivies on the lower bench, or alternate with the rosemaries to give each plant a maximum of light.

At the ends of the bench are large bays. Two more bays stand on the floor. They are best kept out of the sun and do well in these shadowy locations. On the left side of the garden are pots and small flats of culinary herbs. Here grow sage, chives, marjoram, chervil, mints, parsley, sorrel, thyme, and small starts of savory, grouped close together. Beneath the birdbath is a large spreading winter savory, both decorative and useful.

On the right are decorative and fragrant herbs—myrtles, green and sweet-scented, in three-inch pots; large sweet-olive plants that are gradually opening their tiny blossoms, a trailing white-flowered jasmine.

The bright blooms of the elfin herb (*Cuphea hyssopifolia*) are like the tiny flowers in a medieval tapestry. Fragrant creeping thymes, some just moved in from the garden during the January thaw, give evidence of new growth and an old favorite Kenilworth-ivy (*Cymbalaria muralis*), trails down from the shelves.

The accommodating creeping fig (*Ficus pumila*) also decorates these shelves, along with a rosary vine (*Ceropegia*) and a flowering vinca. (*Vinca minor* merits an award for its ability to survive under the most trying conditions.)

There are also some sweet geraniums here that we cannot do without. They are in ten-inch terracotta pots where they are growing into trees. Apple, nutmeg, old spice, and peppermint geraniums also thrive in small pots between the larger plants. Heliotropes, white and purple, dispense their fragrance from hanging baskets and a struggling ice-plant (*Mesembryanthemum crystallinum*) is putting out its pinkish-purple blooms. This is a member of an enormous family of South African herbs whose juice is used in medicines. They are constructed like succulents and survive with almost no water.

Large cardamom plants with long stiffly upright leaves are grouped with the bays because they too like shade. Sweet woodruff in tiny pots grows near them and a coffee-plant with dark-green lustrous leaves. I've started some gray santolinas, too. And several small lady's-mantles here are outgrowing their three-inch pots. They are hardy outdoors, but I like to have them all year because of their fascinating leaves that open like tiny fans.

Culinary climbing nasturtiums in a flat trail down from the shelves and will soon be in bloom. Pots of purple basil are both decorative and flavorsome. The green Italian, or common, basil has been used for seasoning and cut back to sprout again. Seeds of new plants are germinating in pots and will soon be ready to take their place in the window picture. There is also a flat of tarragon and some salad burnet, a charming little plant that is also good for seasoning.

Three kinds of orégano grow in my window garden. They are attractive and fragrant, but I find that the dried Greek orégano has more flavor. Lovage and angelica occupy the shady corner with the bays and cardamoms. They are interesting but need to be supplemented with dried leaves and candied stems for use in recipes. And we must not overlook the Egyptian onions and garlic chives. These are cut constantly but grow back quickly.

Few things are as intriguing to winter visitors as my indoor herb garden. They interrupt almost any conversation to examine the plants, stroke the leaves, and enjoy their odors. Make a guest a nosegay for his buttonhole and he will leave with the feeling that summer lingers here behind the glass.

Choosing the Container

Containers for indoor herbs should be of secondary interest to the plants, and of course of proper size and shape for the specimens they are to hold. Many attractive types are available but pottery is an old stand-by.

Pottery Basket Garden

If space is very limited, I suggest putting all your herbs in one basket. The lovely Italian rosa-type pottery baskets are deep enough to hold sufficient soil and broad enough to accommodate six herbs. Try a planting (shown in the pictures) with a rosemary of the upright type in the center, orange mint and spearmint close to the edge, parsley between the mints, a sweet marjoram behind them, thyme and tarragon in the remaining space.

For an almost sunless window, this small planter can be filled with ivy, which will trail gracefully over the edge, a circle of sweet woodruff, pennyroyal, and one other mint. A good vigorous rosemary will grow for a time without sun, or you could use a lovage or an angelica plant in the center. Sweet cicely is another attractive herb that will grow well with little sun. Bay and myrtle require light only and could be a part of this planting.

The imported Italian pottery basket is not always easy to obtain and represents more of an investment than some will care to make. For these gardeners, cement copies of this charming design are available at nurseries and garden centers where birdbaths are sold.

Clay Pots

Almost all nurserymen today use plastic pots for plants, and for good reasons. They are lightweight, stack easily, are less likely to break, and with the right mixture of potting soil, plants do extremely well in them. On the other hand, they are airtight and there is no drainage through the sides as in a good clay pot. Thus a light potting soil must be used in them, with sand and some vermiculite for drainage.

My personal preference for any window garden is the clay pot. It has a homey outdoor look that harmonizes with plant material, and I believe that plants do better in the home if clay pots are used.

Probably the best pots in the world are of Italian terra rosa, or red clay. They are beautifully shaped with a graceful flare toward the top. The clay is porous but thick so that not too much moisture exudes.

Designing in Pots

Pots for a variety of herbs can be designed in the ways described for the terracotta basket planter. Use a ten-inch pot, preferably of red clay. Place a little soil and some clay shards in the bottom, taking care not to block the drainage hole. Fill the pot half full of soil and set the rosemary in the center as the dominant tall plant. Fill in soil around the roots. Around the rosemary, arrange smaller herbs. I suggest two plants of curled parsley for one side and one orange mint for the other. These will tend to trail over the edge. Or you could use a pineapple mint and a savory, preferably the winter type.

English thyme, a sage, a sweet marjoram, a salad burnet, and a tarragon will grow well together under the same conditions and you may prefer these. Chives are best grown in a separate pot because you will use a lot of them. Basil also does best in a pot of its own, and bay should always be planted separately.

For a ten-inch pot of fragrant herbs, use lemon verbena instead of rosemary, unless you especially want rosemary, which is also fragrant. Or you could select pineapple sage, large and sweet-odored, as the central motif. Set lemon thymes around the edge, and include a lemon balm and an orange mint.

Another suggestion is to make an entire planting of lemon-scented plants. You could use one each of the following: lemon geranium, lemon balm, lemon verbena. For an edging plant lemon thymes, both creeping and vulgaris types.

Built-in Window Planters

Many new homes and apartments have built-in window planters. These are usually intended for tropical plants with decorative leaves, which seem to thrive in them. Unfortunately, drainage is usually provided only by a raised metal strip and there is often no way for stagnant water to drain off.

I have used outside window boxes, cut to measure, in these planters. I filled the boxes with soil and inserted small pots of plants in the earth. This arrangement provides a kind of substitute drainage. Once a week, the inner metal box was lifted out and the planter was drained. A better method is to make two drainage holes in the planter, place a pan underneath, and put soil directly in the planter. Then knock plants out of the pots and insert them in the soil.

Floor Planters

Handsome floor planters are available in many designs. Select one that is deep enough to accommodate the developing roots of your plants. If adequate drainage is not provided, and to arrange for it seems impossible, put a one-inch layer of pot shards in the bottom of the planter, cover this with a layer of sphagnum moss and vermiculite, and add soil. Insert the potted plants in the soil and spread sphagnum moss lightly on top. (The plants should be in small pots, two to four inches.)

Pots keep the roots of plants compact and so provide their own drainage. Water carefully around the stems and keep the soil in the planter moist but not wet.

Strawberry Jar

One of the most attractive planters is the strawberry jar; however, it is too often used to grow plants that are not suited to it. Actually it *is* best for strawberries! These small plants fit in comfortably, grow well with the scant moisture that circulates

A ladder, painted moss-green, and holding pots of geraniums and ivy, makes an unusual plant stand for a big kitchen, family room, or sun porch.

through the jar, and clamber down the sides artistically instead of growing upward. The kind without runners, 'Baron Solemacher', bears well if given enough light to produce bloom. Strawberries with runners will cover the jar completely and produce some fruit and a lot of interesting green foliage.

The succulents are also successful in a strawberry jar. I have a planting of medicinal succulents in one. At the top is a giant *Aloe vera* and down the sides are close-growing kinds such as the houseleeks, or hen-and-chickens. The common houseleek is green, but there are many other interesting types, such as the bearded varieties of *Sempervivum arachnoideum.*

All of these succulents have had herbal uses. The aloe has long been a common plant on windowsills in Sweden, Germany, and other countries of northern Europe. It was probably introduced to England from the Cape of Good Hope by seafaring men. The juice of the aloe was once used to treat skin diseases, burns, and bruises. Today aloes are coming into use again as an ingredient of cosmetics—creams and lipsticks.

Garden on a Tray

Probably everyone who gardens indoors has some favorite form of planting. A tray garden is certainly mine. Many years ago I solved the problem of an herb display, a garden in the smallest possible space that would be practical, attractive, and lasting. I have used trays for many different plantings, and most successfully for the ivy and sweet woodruff ring that surrounds my punch bowl at parties. For display at lectures or as a school exhibit, a tray garden is ideal. If it is properly cared for it will last a long time; one of mine lasted for four years. By that time the rosemaries had grown so large that I had to dismantle the garden and start over again.

The first requirement is a large (twenty-four-inch) metal barrelhead or cover. These covers have a deep indentation around the rim where they lock onto the barrel. This indentation holds

A tray garden will stay fresh and green for months: above left, a 24-inch tray with, right, sphagnum moss and loam ready for planting; center, the tray with 2-inch pots in place; below, the tray after plants have grown and a Saint Francis figure has been placed in the center.

water, and it is essential to plant with the indented side up. Paint the cover with a flat black or dark-green paint and let it dry and air thoroughly.

To plant your garden, have ready: one peach basket (half bushel) of sphagnum moss, one quart of garden loam, and one flat stone about six inches across. Then you will need some variety of well-rooted plants such as this:

1 prostrate rosemary
1 ten-inch rosemary
1 winter savory (about four inches)
2 common thymes
1 lemon thyme
1 culinary thyme
1 orégano
2 sweet marjorams
4 purple basils
1 orange mint
1 spearmint
1 peppermint
6 creeping thymes
2 English pennyroyals
4 sweet woodruffs
4 parsleys
3 garlic chives

Planting the Tray

Place wet sphagnum moss over the entire surface of the barrelhead and put a rock in the center. Sprinkle garden loam through this first layer of sphagnum. Add a second layer of loam, building it up over the rock.

Knock the plants from their pots. (They should first be well watered but not wet.) Place the ten-inch rosemary in the center behind the rock and the prostrate rosemary beside it, lifting both so that they are higher than the space surrounding them. Plant the savory behind the rosemary, a common thyme on either side, orégano and sweet marjoram between the thymes, garlic chives toward the center because they may grow tall, orange mint and spearmint near the rim with parsley, at the edge creeping thyme, alternated with creeping pennyroyal and sweet woodruff.

Cover all roots carefully with sphagnum and a spoonful of soil and pack more soil around them if necessary. Water the garden with a weak solution of Rapid-Gro or other good liquid fertilizer. Keep the garden out of the sun until the plants have absorbed the moisture—about three days. Don't allow water to stand in the tray except in the shallow outside ring, because this container has no drainage except that provided by the sphagnum. The moss acts like a sponge, and unless flooded it prevents an accumulation of water. If the plants do not absorb all excess moisture, carefully tilt the tray and drain it off.

I like to place a small figure of St. Francis in the center of the rock, with the rosemary for a background; a figure of St. Fiacre, patron saint of gardeners, is also appropriate. I change the ornament with the seasons and just now have an iron birdbath shell in the center with small ceramic birds around it.

Alternative Designs

There are other ways to plant this little indoor herb garden. I have omitted chives, which are too sprawling, and other plants that do not seem to like this setting. Some of the gray herbs could be substituted—sage near the rosemary, gray santolina on the side opposite the prostrate rosemary, two shrubs of *Ruta graveolens* 'Blue Beauty' as sentinels on either side of the figure. The culinary herbs included here would be rosemary, savory, thyme, woodruff, mint, and orégano.

Care of Tray Garden

A shallow planting of this kind needs feeding every two weeks with liquid fertilizer, a soaking once a month in the sink, and a thorough cleansing of the leaves with a bulb syringe or other hand sprayer. It requires sun part of the day. The mints will need watching to keep them from overrunning the planting. To con-

How to plant a hanging basket: Above, line the basket with moss and pour in a proper soil mixture; below, place the plants, here rose geranium, ivy, and thyme; and the result after some weeks of growing.

Above, a terra-cotta hanging basket makes an excellent container for the sprawling growth of the peppermint geranium, *Pelargonium tomentosum*. Below, a planter box (shown in cross section, with pots set on a layer of stones) holds, along the back: mint, garlic chives, winter savory, and rosemary; in front: thyme, sweet marjoram, and parsley.

Lovage, sweet woodruff, pennyroyal, and peppermint in a lovely terra-cotta Italian basket

A ten-inch pot of mixed herbs, with rosemary for height in the center

Parsley, savory, and rosemary in pots suspended in lettuce baskets

A pebble tray with pots of calamondin orange, sweet-olive, and lemon verbena

trol them, cut the straying root ends as they spread. If the soil becomes sour, sprinkle lime over it and water it in well. Be careful not to let the herbs dry out; both the earth and the cover around them is shallow. Once plants are rooted in and have shown new growth, they will not require as much attention.

Incidentally, a tray garden always gives pleasure to the aged and the handicapped. It can be set on a table with a sheet of glass underneath to protect the finish. There it is readily accessible to a person who cannot move about easily.

For Hanging Baskets

Some trailing plants will probably be in order for your garden window. Heliotropes are excellent for hanging baskets. I like both white- and purple-flowered species and am careful always to take cuttings from the most fragrant plants. They do vary. It is a good idea to choose your heliotropes personally because there are stunning varieties with big handsome flowers that are scentless. Heliotrope is included in the herb window only because of its fragrance. It has no practical use.

Emergency Planting

Many garden enthusiasts buy their herbs early in the year—often at the big flower shows—with the idea of transferring them later to a summer garden. The problem is where to put them in the meantime.

The tiny plants must remain in their starting pots for several months if they are to grow well, and the collection may be rather extensive. For emergency housing, an outdoor window box can save the day.

Bring the box inside, make drainage holes in the bottom with a hammer and nail, and fill to within three inches of the top with potting soil. Insert the pots of herbs well down in the soil and cover the surface of planter and pots with a thick layer of sphagnum moss. The moss makes an attractive topping and holds water like a sponge. It keeps the upper roots from burning and is good protection against excessive indoor heat and dryness.

To prevent damage to the windowsill from drainage, put heavy aluminum foil, a sheet of glass, or a pan under the window box. Check the drainage holes frequently to be sure that they are open. This planting is strictly utilitarian. Even so, it is interesting to watch.

2

Health for Herbs Indoors—Basic Culture

To grow herbs indoors successfully, select your plants carefully and provide the basic culture for each species. Some herbs that are desirable in an outdoor garden are unsuitable indoors because of their size or unattractive habit of growth.

Selecting the Plants

In selecting herbs for indoor growing, you can avoid disappointment by ruling out certain types. Don't plant annuals or perennials that will spread and take over your entire space, or weak kinds that will die miserably. Avoid, unless you are extremely curious about them, herbs that are grown for their seed-producing heads. To get enough seeds for flavoring, you need a long garden row. Avoid also herbs that must be grown from seeds that are slow to germinate. This eliminates four herbs in the first part of an alphabetical list: anise, caraway, coriander, and cumin. Caraway needs to be three feet high to produce good umbels of seed.

Purchased Plants

When buying plants, make certain that they are well rooted. If roots are beginning to show through the drainage hole in the pot, the plants should be repotted or put in a planter. Don't buy dry plants; geraniums and thymes will usually revive but rosemaries never. If your purchases are made in the early spring, woody plants such as lemon verbena may be just coming out of a dormant period and will show only one or two green leaves. If so, look for a sturdy stalk that is firm in the pot.

Examine the underside of leaves, and the stems, for aphids and white fly which are sometimes found on plants that have not been sprayed carefully. These pests are not fatal; they can be removed easily with Black Leaf 40 or malathion.

Large plants are not necessarily the best selection. Look for growth that is crisp and healthy.

Selection also involves choosing the right plants for the window that is available. Many herbs need sun and languish without it; others grow well with good light and very little sun. A few will do well without sun, but all must have some kind of light. Without natural light, Gro Lamps are necessary.

Plants that will grow in a sunless window include: angelica (*A. archangelica*), chervil (*Anthriscus cerefolium*), English ivy (*Hedera helix*), lovage (*Levisticum officinale*), lemon balm (*Melissa*), mints (*Mentha*), spiderwort (*Tradescantia*), sweet cicely (*Myrrhis odorata*), and sweet woodruff (*Asperula odorata*). Rosemary will sometimes adjust to a northwest window with no sun. Myrtle (*Myrtus communis*) grows if the light is good but not very bright. Bay (*Laurus nobilis*) should thrive.

If your space is limited, decide whether you want a culinary window garden or just a group of fragrant plants. Among culinary herbs the most successful for indoors (with some reservations that will be mentioned under plant descriptions) are such sturdy growers as basil, chives, winter savory, mints, tarragon, rosemary, and thyme.

Tools and Materials

For indoor gardening you will need the following tools: a small trowel, pocket-size pruners, and a misting bulb or fogger. You will also need certain materials: sphagnum moss, vermiculite, potting soil, an insecticide, liquid fertilizer, and lime. These supplies can be bought at garden centers.

Sphagnum moss is invaluable. It is an antiseptic and absorbent swamp material. A small bag, preferably of the long grain type, will do. Get a one- to ten-pound bag of vermiculite, a micaceous material, just a little lime, and potting soil as required—if you do not mix your own. For an insecticide use Black Leaf 40 or malathion without DDT.

Light and Temperature

Dry indoor heat is detrimental to many plants that can stand burning sun and drought in an outdoor garden. Pot conditions are entirely different from ground plantings. When plants are in the ground, the sun or heat hits only the tops of the plants; their roots are in the cool earth. Plants in pots are vulnerable to the sun or heat on all sides and dry out much more quickly. Hot dry air should be mitigated, although sun is often necessary. I find a small deep birdbath, filled with water, both decorative and useful. It helps keep the air moist and even in our relatively cool farmhouse needs filling every second day.

Room heat may drop as low as forty degrees at night and through the day rise as high as seventy to eighty degrees in the sun without damage to plants as long as moisture is maintained. An even heat of fifty to sixty degrees is the ideal of many enthusiasts. Plants, like people, enjoy fresh air but drafts should be avoided. Old houses with their loose windows provide just the right amount of air. In modern houses, a bedroom window is sometimes best for herbs that like a cool situation. Halls, if they have sunlight, are excellent and basement windows or glassed-in bulkheads are possible locations for large plants.

Watering

Proper watering is really the prime factor in making your garden thrive. Too much has been said about keeping house plants on the dry side. If drainage is good, house plants should almost always be watered every day, or at least checked. Water all herbs from the top, not the bottom. Preferably water them in the late morning. If this is not possible, water them early in the morning. Avoid as a rule watering herbs at night, but if plants have been forgotten and are dry, a night soaking is better than letting them go until the next day. Night watering tends to develop molds and other fungus troubles. There is not a doubt that rainwater is the best in the world for plants, but most people consider it unavailable! Luckily, herbs seem to adjust themselves to tap water (warm to cool) without difficulty.

We suggest top watering because most of the herbs like to have their leaves sprayed. Spraying them with water removes the dust which can cling to large leaves and disfigure them. If it is not possible to spray the leaves in the window where the plants are growing, take the plants to the kitchen sink and give them a treat. With a fine faucet spray or syringe, thoroughly wash both sides of the leaves.

The only herbs that will tolerate consistently wet feet are the mints. Excess water must be drained from the others through the holes in the pots so that roots do not stand in water for any length of time. Foliar feeding once a month can be combined with the spray watering.

Soil Mixtures

If you buy your herbs at a reliable nursery they will doubtless be potted in a proper soil mixture. However, since we expect these plants to grow on and be repotted, it is a good idea to have your own soil mixture at hand. If plant soil becomes sour or packed, your herbs will benefit from repotting. Discard the top layer and add fresh soil. The classic mixture—three parts garden loam, one part peat moss, and two parts sand—drains well and needs only the addition of lime to turn a rather acid mix to the sweet soil that many herbs demand. A teaspoon of lime to a five-inch pot would not be too much. If you are not in a position to mix soil, you can buy both acid and alkaline soils at a garden center.

Drainage

I have one prime requirement for pots, tubs, and planters that are to contain herbs: absolute and complete drainage from the top through an opening in the bottom. Drainage stones in a container without such a hole are not enough. Stagnant water collects in the bottom and causes the roots to die.

I realize that this requirement presents a problem to the housekeeper who visualizes her herbs in some favorite container that cannot be violated with a drill. The sweet little china pots with different herbs painted on them are usually too small to be practical, and are not porous; many have no drainage holes.

I once purchased some huge terracotta tubs from a firm in Italy. They were fabulously expensive by the time they arrived, and very beautiful. I filled them outdoors with scented geraniums. The geraniums grew well for about a month, then yellow leaves appeared, the plants started to droop, and died. Checking the tubs, I found the soil soggy at the bottom. I tried again, using drainage materials such as broken pots, stones, and sand. That was not successful either.

Drilling holes in the bottom, even at the risk of breaking the tubs, seemed the only solution. Although the material was thick and unyielding, this was done successfully, and from that time on there was no trouble. Through the years, geraniums, lemon verbenas, orange trees, myrtles, and bays have grown happily in these handsome tubs.

If you want to use decorative jardiniers, don't plant directly in them, but keep plants in pots and check frequently for the collection of stagnant water.

Transplanting from the Garden

If you are bringing herbs from the outdoors for your window garden, don't wait until frost threatens. In New England, October

1 is usually the outside time to pot scented geraniums. Pineapple sage and all the tender sages should be potted and ready for shelter by the fifteenth of September. If they are potted and the pots dug back into the ground, they will be ready for quick exit from the garden when cold weather is predicted. Rosemaries, bays, and myrtles are often safe and happy in the garden until November 1, but it is a good idea to bring them inside by mid-October. All potted plants need extra watering when they first come in. Give these three plants a good watering every day.

The plants that will not survive frost and require indoor protection during winter, in addition to those we have listed, include the fragrant olive, the basils, marjorams, orégano, dittany, nasturtiums, jasmines, fennel (except the bronze variety), heliotrope, myrtle (*Myrtus communis*), lemon verbena, and variegated lemon thymes (except *Thymus aureus citriodorus*). Pot marigolds should be brought in for color as well as safety.

When Plants Come Indoors

Mature plants must not be allowed to dry out at any time when they are first brought in from the garden. Outdoor herbs, first brought inside, look so healthy that it is easy to forget how vulnerable they are. *Thorough* watering once a day is absolutely necessary. It is essential during hot, dry, and very sunny periods to check them for dryness again in the early afternoon, and water again if necessary. Spray tops freely with water and a good liquid fertilizer.

Immediately before the transfer from garden to house, plants should be sprayed for aphids, white fly, and red spider mites. Malathion is one of the least lethal of the poison sprays and leaves no residue. Black Leaf 40 is also safe and can be alternated with malathion if either insecticide loses its effectiveness. Organic gardeners who object to even these mild sprays may use a weak solution of yellow naphtha soap.

When plants are first potted, lay them on their sides in a

As decorative touches, flowering and highly scented herbs make a pleasing display in apothecary jars: left, the elfin herb *Cuphea hyssopifolia;* right, African baby's-breath *Chaenostoma fastigatum.*

potting shed or on the floor of the garage and spray them thoroughly. (If you spray them indoors keep a window open.) One of the new glass force-sprays that can be attached to a hose is the easiest to use. Lacking this, a bulb syringe will do. Be sure to spray the undersides of leaves as well as the top surfaces.

Transplanting Seedlings

For the successful transplanting of small seedlings raised out of doors (rosemaries, sage, parsley, marjoram, basil), use two- or three-inch pots. Take the pots to the garden, place the plants in them, and cover their roots with the soil in which they have grown. Next dig a small trench, insert the pots, and spread mulch. Keep plants well watered; don't allow them to dry out even once. When roots crowd the edge of the pots, transplant to pots of a size desired for the window garden, but not overlarge in proportion to the root ball, of course. Knock the pots sharply against a table or step and the roots will slip out easily with a ball of soil that is easily transferred to another pottery medium for growth during the winter.

In purchased herbs adequate root growth has already been developed and the potted nursery plants are rarely offered to customers directly from outside rows. Plants are potted well in advance of winter and the wilting that was so disastrous in the past is avoided.

Taking Cuttings and Rooting Perennials

A precious plant is always worth propagating. This is insurance, important to your continuing success and pleasure. Always take cuttings from well-grown, healthy specimens. Herbs that tend to become rangy outdoors benefit from top-branch cuts. Don't use the soft forced growth that develops when plants have too little light and too much heat and water. Cut this pale growth back to the main woody stem and discard it. Take cuttings from firm growth with either a straight or a slanting cut. I never take a cutting less than three inches long, although many use one-and-a-half-inch cuts successfully.

A small deep flat with bottom drainage makes a good bed for a few cuttings. A plastic "pony" flat is also suitable, but handle it carefully lest it crack on the side. A piece of clear plastic wrapped around the outside of a flat, cut with a flap that can be pulled over the top, helps hold these flats together. Make a few holes on the flap for air. Don't plug the drainage holes or the propagating mixture will become soggy.

For a propagation medium, mix two parts of sand (sifted building sand will do) with one part of vermiculite. Moisten this mixture thoroughly. Let the water drain through, then press out the remaining water. The medium is now ready for the cuttings.

Inserting the Cuttings

Keep the cuttings cool and shaded while the transfer is being made to the rooting flat, but don't put the slips in water. Insert the cuttings in the medium. Don't crowd them. Remove lower leaves so that the inserted portion will be free of green growth. About one third of the cutting should be in the soil. Leaves are needed on the above-ground portion to promote life while the cutting is growing roots.

Few herbs will root in water. True mint, spearmint, orange mint, and apple mint are exceptions. The planting medium I have is generally preferable for all cuttings.

Herbs that can be propagated from root cuttings include basil, catnip, horehound, rosemaries, savory, true myrtles, pineapple sage, verbenas, germanders, thymes (although it is often easier to pull out a root from the many that form), lemon balm, southernwood and all artemesias, tarragon, and garden sage.

Some of the most desirable herbs root so poorly and take such an interminable time to do it that it is better to purchase small plants than to struggle with cuttings. Among these are the bays which usually take about six months to grow two small feeble roots, and lemon verbena, which is exceedingly difficult to root.

The usual length of time required to root cuttings is four to six weeks for lemon balm, thyme, basil, peppermint, spearmint, orange and apple mints. Cuttings from plants with woody stems are apt to root more slowly—rosemary, myrtle, artemesia, santolina, and germander. Members of the mint family root quickly.

Keep the cuttings in the flats well watered. Don't move them until they have roots one quarter to one half an inch long.

Potting Cuttings

When roots have formed, cuttings take on a bright look even though new leaves have not appeared. You can make certain that they have rooted by carefully spooning the soil from one side, or by lifting one out from the medium very gently.

Transfer rooted cuttings into two-inch pots. Soak plastic pots briefly to remove any residue. If clay pots have been used for other plants, scrub them well in hot water, then soak them until the clay is saturated. Moisten your potting soil and fill the pots one quarter full. Let some of the original propagating soil cling to the roots. If it drops off, sprinkle a teaspoonful of it around the roots. Add soil to within one inch of the top of the pot, and firm it gently around the transplants. Don't water them immediately. (The soil is already moist.)

Set newly potted plants in a shaded area or shade them with a newspaper. Keep them out of the sun for one week, or until growth starts. The soil should be kept moist but not wet. Don't place pots on a wet surface, on stones or gravel. To retain moisture, set them in a metal tray packed with moist (not wet) sand or vermiculite.

Leave the pots in this tray until roots begin to show through the drainage holes. Then, plants should be repotted. When repotting them, follow the same procedure as the transfer of cuttings. Make sure that soil is moist and drained. Transfer plants to three-inch, or at most four-inch, containers. A few pieces of broken clay pot or some small stones in the bottom of the container will keep the opening in the bottom clear for drainage.

Fill pots one third full and transfer plants with a ball of earth. These plants can now be placed in the sun. Since they are growing actively, they will need more water and there is less danger of their stems and leaves rotting. If the tops grow too tall, trim them sparingly.

When very large plants are potted directly from the garden, there is always a chance of loss because roots must be reduced for potting and plants sometimes find it difficult to adjust to new conditions and surroundings. You can take cuttings from large plants in August, root them in sand and vermiculite, and pot the resulting plants for indoors rather than jeopardize the large parent plants by potting. Cutting works well with geraniums but not always with other plants. Large rosemaries, bays, myrtles, and lemon verbenas are valuable enough to be given the attention they need to hold them over for another year in their largest size in the garden.

Tips for the Unwary

Window planters are often built over ducts, radiators, or floor vents, where heat dries out roots and blasts foilage of species that require cool conditions. Be careful in your selection. Few herbs can stand this. Look for another location.

Plants suspended in the air or placed on stands dry out quickly because they are exposed to currents of hot air on all sides and to the sun. Give them daily attention; water them generously. Few herbs survive when their roots are exposed in a ring-pot planting.

If a plant shelf is crowded, turn the pots frequently. Whole sides of rosemaries will brown off if they are pressed against a wall or another plant. Turn them once a week. If a mixture of herbs is contained in a large pot, be sure to turn it.

Clip browned leaves from plants whenever they appear.

Don't overfertilize herbs. Three applications during the winter are enough.

Make sure containers are large enough for expanding plant roots.

If leaves drop, check for aphids or white fly. Persistent losses could indicate a leaking gas jet.

Follow individual needs for trimming plants. Some need constant cutting to prevent leggy growth.

Most casualties occur when plants are first brought in from the garden. Select pots of the right size. Roots should not touch the sides of the pot. If roots are crowded, the tips of a plant will brown within a few weeks.

Scented geraniums grow so enormously during a single season that they have far too much top for the root systems when brought indoors. Trim the tops drastically, leaving only the lower leaves. Put the trimmed plants in four- to six-inch containers.

3

Herbs to Grow for Flavor

Herbs add zest and flavor to drinks, canapés, entrees, soups, salads, and desserts. When winter puts the outdoor garden to sleep, pots of culinary herbs in the window remind you that spring will come again, while offering their leaves for that special touch in cookery.

It is impossible to put herbs into exact categories. Some that are important for flavor are also fragrant, ornamental, and fun to grow. Many have a centuries-old history in medicine and magic. As I list the various plants for seasoning, I shall mention other uses and recount some of the legends associated with them.

Pungent and indispensable in the kitchen, the alliums come first. For indoor growing, I recommend chives, garlic chives, Egyptian onions, and leeks.

Allium Species

According to a Mohammedan legend, "When Satan stepped out of the Garden of Eden, garlick sprang up from the spot where he placed his left foot, and onions where his right foot touched."

Garlic and onions, in picturesque settings, provide a decorative note in a kitchen, and such displays are also practical. They may or may not exorcise witches and protect the family against the evil eye but they are handy, certainly for the cook.

The younger Pliny wrote that garlic and onions were considered deities by the Egyptians and were invoked to seal an oath or a bargain. Allium species were important items of food at ancient Roman banquets, but were also used in quantity by the common people. Strong alliums were given to wrestlers, laborers, and race horses to give them strength. In medieval times, garlic was considered an antidote for sunstroke. Today its most popular use, outside the kitchen, is to drive away garden moles; all alliums are good for this.

Chives, *Allium schoenoprasum*

Chives grow wild in Greece and Italy and some are found in Europe and parts of Asia. The botanical name means "rush-leek" and refers to the fine rushlike leaves. Chives are a favorite seasoning, one of the most useful of all indoor herbs.

The Plant

For potting, young but mature plants are best. Side roots from larger crowns can be divided and planted, about eight or ten to a pot. Cut the long scapes back to the crown because they become yellow and lax when moved. I suggest that chives be potted outside and left to freeze before you bring them into the house. Freezing provides a rest period and the resultant growth is firm and fresh. Starting from seed is not usually satisfactory because it takes nearly two years for plants to mature. Three well-filled pots of chives will not be too many because this herb is used in more dishes than any other herb except parsley.

Indoors it grows to a height of eight inches.

Its Uses

Cut and use chives often. This keeps the plant growing and the new growth will be tender and sweet. Cut it fine and add it to soups, salads, cream-cheese mixes, omelets, meats, and mashed potatoes. The purple flowers are famous in flower cookery and are an exotic addition to omelets and scrambled eggs.

Egyptian or Top Onion, *Allium cepa viviparum*

The Egyptian onion has been known in different forms since early times but the type we grow today probably was brought from France to Canada, where it was popular in the nineteenth century.

The Plant

The plant is perpetuated by small brown bulblets that form at the tip of a central stem. These bulblets can be planted or used in seasoning. Bulbs that form underground become soft as the tops develop and are not as good for seasoning as the small top onions.

You will need at least six plants if you want to use them in cooking. Let one plant go to seed and use the top onions to extend your supply. Plant in a bulb pan in porous but moderately rich soil. Water well but do not allow soil to stay wet. A little sand or vermiculite around the bulbs helps keep them firm and healthy.

This onion grows to a height of ten to twelve inches indoors.

Its Uses

Cut the green tops as they grow and add them to soups and salads. Chopped fine, they are good for canapés. Or sauté them in butter with rice. The strong-flavored small onions can be used as a seasoning. Sometimes they are pickled for cocktails. The tops assume fantastic shapes as they develop. When mature, they can be used in flower arrangements.

Garlic Chives, or Oriental Garlic, *Allium tuberosum*

Garlic chives is a wild plant of eastern Asia, a favorite herb in China and Japan. The whole plant is eaten raw and the flowers are used in salads.

The Plant

Outdoors, this edible lily spreads rapidly from self-sown seed and grows one to two feet tall. Indoors, in pots, it remains small—about eight to ten inches. Grown in a tub, however, it would attain its full height of eighteen to twenty-four inches.

It resembles common chives but leaves are flat rather than rounded. The panicle of white, starlike, very fragrant flowers smells like tuberoses. When cultivated and fertilized, the inflorescence becomes larger and can be used in flower arrangements. Used individually, the blossoms are effective in miniature flower arrangements. You will need four to six plants to have enough for seasoning experiments.

Its Uses

Cut the stems as you do chives. The entire tender stem and leaves of young plants can be chopped into a salad, added to cream-cheese mixes, or eaten raw like scallions.

Leek, *Allium porrum*

The leek is of uncertain origin but is probably native to Mediterranean countries. It has been used extensively in Egypt from the time of the pyramids. It is the national plant of Wales, where according to legend it once saved the country by furnishing food for a beleaguered garrison.

The Plant

In our climate, outdoors, the leek takes two years to mature from seed. Inside, seeds can be sown at any time, and usable plants should be produced in a year. It is really better to buy a flat of six to eight plants that grow twelve to eighteen inches high. Even this number would not provide many for culinary use. Grow them as an interesting experiment and to provide small amounts of seasoning.

Leeks grown in a tub can be wintered outside on a terrace in their second year. There they will produce the wonderful purple seed head with a thin cap covering them. To watch this cap lift and move to a rakish angle as the seeds develop is fascinating. It finally disappears altogether, exposing the round seed head. This can be cut with a long stem and dried for flower arranging or the seeds can be sown for new plants.

Its Uses

The entire stalk is cut down to the blanched white lower part. Chop it into a soup or use it in cock-a-leekie, a famous Scottish dish. Stalks can be blanched in butter or boiled and eaten like asparagus.

Basil, *Ocimum*

Basil, an annual, is native to India, where it is dedicated to the deities Krishna and Vishnu. It is grown in many Hindu homes and is thought to purify the air and bless the household. It is carried to the funeral pyre as a passport to heaven.

The name "basil" has two possible sources. One account claims it was derived from the word *basileus* meaning "king," perhaps because it was used as a royal medicine. John Parkinson, a seventeenth-century writer on plants suggests that it was considered the king of fragrant herbs. The most accepted story associates it with scorpions and a fierce fabulous creature called a basilisk that could kill with a look.

Basil was once a courting herb. A sprig of it in a young man's hat or in a maiden's hand bespoke affection. However, it was also a symbol of hate, and the Greeks used it to represent poverty and disgrace. Probably no plant has had a more controversial background, but everyone agrees on its sweet spicy odor.

The Plant

Bring in seedlings from the garden and pinch back centers to the first set of leaves. A new top will grow quickly and the plant will bush out attractively. This technique keeps blossoms from forming and prolongs life. Basil needs to be well watered, and liquid fertilizer once a month is beneficial.

It grows to a height of two feet.

For indoor cultivation, the type generally listed as common, sometimes as Italian, is most successful. Purple, the 'Dark Opal' variety, makes a very good house plant. It reacts well to warm growing conditions and will thrive indefinitely if blossoms are not allowed to form. Like all annuals, basils run quickly to seed and this sometimes ends a productive life.

Lettuce leaf (*O. crispum*), the Japanese basil, is fine to grow but requires more room and its large succulent leaves attract mites. The miniature bushy types are attractive and easy to grow from seed but do not yield as much for cutting as common basil (*O. basilicum*). Two of the bush varieties have a strong lemon odor and are particularly sweet and spicy. The sacred basil of India, holy basil, can be grown from seed. It is an interesting plant historically but is not good for seasoning.

Its Uses

Pinch out the tops for general use. New ones will appear within a week and the process can be repeated. The use of this plant in spaghetti sauce is well known. It is good in salads, a must with tomatoes, and an ingredient of many dried all-purpose seasonings. Add green and purple leaves to vinegar for color and flavor. The result is a pink liquid attractive in appearance and excellent in taste.

Bay, laurel, *Laurus nobilis*

Bay leaves once formed the crowns worn by poets, Roman emperors, and Delphic oracles. A crown of bay leaves was a mark of distinction and the origin of our modern academic term "bachelor." It derives from *bacca-laureus,* laurel berry. Bay was reputed to protect houses and people from the ravages of thunderstorms.

The Plant

The true seasoning bay is a south European native and grows outdoors to twenty-five or thirty feet; indoors it grows three to six feet tall, but only after many years.

It is often trimmed into decorative shapes and used as a formal plant at the approaches to Italian villas.

Bay grows slowly and its roots are so long in forming that propagation by cuttings is discouraging. Plants for potting and sale are usually one to two years old. Therefore they cost more than any other culinary herb. Plan to repot your bay as soon as roots fill the container, and add new soil each time. After two years it will grow comparatively rapidly. Scale insects seem to be the plant's only enemy. Scale looks like small brown dots on the underside of the leaves. To remove them on small plants scrub them off with a stiff brush, such as a toothbrush, dipped in soap suds. Large plants may need spraying with an insecticide.

Plan to give bays some shade because leaves burn out quickly in hot sun and lose their luster and rich dark color. Never let them dry out.

Its Uses

Cut leaves from the side of the plant unless it has grown too tall. Then take tip growth. Add a leaf when cooking shrimp or other shellfish. Use it to flavor soups, sauces, and curries. Include it in Christmas wreaths and other decorations.

Burnet, *Sanguisorba minor*

Burnet is no doubt a Mediterranean native but it has become naturalized in the dry chalky downs of England. It has been tried as a forage crop, being highly nutritious and evergreen in pastures where soil is poor and weed competition not too great. The old Greek name *poterium* refers to its use in wine cups, where it imparted a cool cucumber flavor. It was used in much the same way as borage and (combined with wine) explains the saying "burnet for the merry heart."

Bacon, in his famous essay on gardens, suggests that burnet be set with mints and wild thyme "to perfume the air most delightfully, being trodden on and crushed."

The Plant

Burnet is an attractive little perennial with deep-green serrated leaves, often with reddish stems. The flower is purplish red and the seeds germinate readily. Burnet likes very dry soil, really poor ground, and this must be remembered in potting it for indoor growing. Give it a sandy soil, add a little lime to the pot, and place it where it will get as much sun as possible.

It grows from one to two feet tall outdoors and ultimately forms a large clump. Indoors growth is smaller and more lax. I suggest potting it in a shallow rather than a deep pot. Select seedlings from the garden, because the long taproot of older clumps is difficult to transfer. Put three to six seedlings in a five-by-seven-inch flat. You will need two flats to get enough for practical use.

Its Uses

Cut leaves for flavoring from young plants; the leaves of older plants are likely to be tough. I like to pick the fernlike fronds that come up in the center of the circle of leaves because they are always tender and tasty.

The odor and flavor of burnet are like cucumber. Add burnet to sweet butter for a canapé spread or for "cucumber" sandwiches. It is also good in cream-cheese mixes. Let these stand overnight in the refrigerator for best results. Burnet is also good in salads with chopped chives.

Calendula, *Calendula officinalis*, pot marigold

A pleasant old-fashioned flower, the calendula was widely cherished in the past for the color it added to gardens, as a seasoning, and as a medicine. It is an annual in our climate and is native from the Canary Islands to Persia. Shakespeare wrote of "the marigold that goes to bed with the sun and with him rises weeping."

The small Mediterranean species with brilliant orange flowers was grown for medicine, for tea, and as a salve. The "sovereign virtues" mentioned by Fuller suggest that it was a specific for headache, jaundice, red eyes, and ague. The "dried flowers were used to comfort and strengthen the hart," wrote the *Countrie Farm* in 1699. Grocers and spice dealers kept barrels of dried petals "in so much that no broths were well made without dried marigold." Just to look at this bright sun symbol was enough to cure "evil humors."

The Plant

The leaves were boiled as a pot herb, hence the name pot marigold. The early single variety *C. officinalis* closes its petals at night and opens them with the sun.

Bring in small plants from outdoor beds for your window garden or buy a flat of six to eight well-started seedlings. Standard potting soil, not heavily fertilized, is best, and a four- to six-inch pot or bulb pan makes a good container.

If plants are brought in from the garden, cut back their top growth, place in a cool spot, and wait for new growth before bringing them to your indoor garden. If you have an outdoor garden, sow seeds in July or August for small seedlings to transplant.

Indoors it grows ten to fourteen inches high.

Pick flowers frequently to keep blooms coming, and cut off seed heads as fast as they form.

Its Uses

The flowers are edible and are tremendously decorative in salads. A salad decorated with calendulas and nasturtiums is a beautiful sight. Use the petals in soups and stews and also in tea.

Catnip, *Nepeta cataria*

Catnip is a perennial of the mint family with soft hairy leaves resembling apple mint. The leaves are somewhat heart-shaped and toothed. The gray-blue flowers, in dense whorls on short stalks, dry quickly and turn gray.

The plant is naturalized in England, where it is considered a native, and in some parts of New England. It was brought to America by the colonists not because cats loved it but because a good wholesome tea could be brewed from its leaves. Catnip tea was once popular in English country places when the cost of China tea was prohibitive. It is said that chewing catnip will make the gentlest person quarrelsome and that rats will not go near a place that smells of this herb. Catnip tea has been used medicinally for colds, particularly for children's colds, and as a remedy for fever. It has been recommended also for hysteria, headaches, and nightmares.

The Plant

An attractive plant for indoor growing because of its gray foliage, catnip is quite undemanding. The only protection it needs is from the family cats. It seldom intrigues them when it is green and growing, but if it has any dried leaves, look out. Sun is good for it, but it does well in any spot where there is light.

It grows indoors to a height of twelve to eighteen inches.

Its Uses

Cut the leaves for curing as the plants mature and branch out, and hang them in a warm dry place. For catnip tea, crumble dried leaves and use one teaspoon to a cup. Brew it in a tightly covered teapot for at least ten minutes. Do not boil your tea. This impairs its flavor and its effectiveness as a medicine. A few dried leaves or a small bag of them will amuse your cat. After playing with it for a while, he will tear it to pieces.

Dill, *Anethum graveolens*

A native Mediterranean plant, dill was once used by magicians to cast spells, and by possible victims to protect them from such chicanery. It was also used as a medicine to induce sleep.

The Plant

Dill has feathery green foliage, branched along a single stalk. It grows up to two feet high and sets an umbel which contains the seeds used in pickling. It resembles fennel in foliage and seed head but has its own characteristic growth, taste, and odor. It is best to grow them as window-garden plants for their foliage, which is today more highly prized than the seeds.

Dill likes a rather rich well-drained soil. It can be grown from seed in peat pots then transferred to clay pots or small flats. A dozen dill plants will not be too many and some dill seed might be planted to keep them coming because the life of this plant is not long.

Its Uses

Cut the green leaves, known commercially as dill weed, and use them with fish—particularly shellfish—with boiled or mashed potatoes, and in salads, vinegar, and pickles.

Fennel, *Foeniculum vulgare*, Bronze Fennel, Florence Fennel

Fennel, a native of Europe, was once esteemed highly for food, medicine, and magic. "The leaves, seeds and rootes are both for meat and medicine," John Parkinson wrote in 1640; "the Italians especially doe much delight in the use thereof and therefore transplant and whiten it. . . . We use it to lay upon fish or to boil it therewith and with divers other things, as also the seeds in bread."

William Coles wrote in *Nature's Paradise* in 1650: "Both the seeds, leaves and the roots . . . are much used in drinks and broths for those that are grown too fat, to abate their unwieldiness and cause them to grow more gaunt and lank."

Earlier herbalists believed that fennel could restore eyesight and give protection against witchcraft. The Greeks believed that it induced longevity, strength, and courage.

The Plant

All varieties of fennel grow reasonably well indoors. Put them in the sun; water them moderately. A window-box planting could consist of eight to ten plants. Grow them for their leaves, not for seed. You can buy seeds for seasoning at a grocery or drugstore, where they are sold to make a soothing tea for babies.

Of the perennial fennels, the sturdiest and best is the handsome bronze variety, whose leaves are used for seasoning and decoration. Bronze fennel will continue after the annual type has lived its life and departed. Include this herb in a planter, or grow it in a separate pot. Three bronze fennels should yield ample cuttings, and six to eight plants of the green Florence kind would be worthwhile.

Indoors it grows about ten to fifteen inches high.

Its Uses

Chop "weed," or green leaves, and use them in salads, with fish, or with fennel seed in a cream-cheese spread.

Marjoram, *Majorana hortensis* or *Origanum majorana* (Linnaeus), sweet marjoram, knotted marjoram

Marjoram, a member of the *Origanum* family, greatly resembles orégano. It symbolizes blushes and happiness. In the past it was used as a tea, with lemon balm as a fragrant furniture polish, and as a strewing herb. Its leaves filled the sweet bags of the past and it was used also in "washing waters" and "swete powders."

The Plant

Sweet marjoram is an attractive little plant with rounded light-green leaves and (indoors) a rather lax habit of growth. It comes easily from seed, although sometimes damping off causes disaster. A light coating of shredded sphagnum moss will prevent this. If plants are brought in from the garden, separate them carefully so that there will not be too many in a pot. They need sunlight and air space for health and proper growth. Wash their leaves frequently.

Marjoram grows indoors about six to eight inches high.

Its Uses

Cut leaves from the top of the plant to prevent blossoming. Use them in soups, with lamb, in stuffing mixtures, and with sausage, pork, duck, eggs, and vegetables.

Nasturtium, *Tropaeolum*, Indian Cress

The flowering nasturtium is native to the New World, growing wild from Mexico to Peru. With many other plants known to the Indians, it was taken to Europe after the conquest and recipes soon featured both its leaves and flowers. During the seventeenth and eighteenth centuries the flowers were featured in floral salads while the leaves were used like water cress. Pickled seeds doubled for capers.

The Plant

For growing nasturtium indoors use a small pot or box of potting soil. Soak the seeds overnight to soften their hard shells and hasten germination. Press them into the soil, water them well, and keep the box or pot in a warm shaded place until the seeds sprout.

The plants bloom well in a northern exposure but are also at home in full sun. Poor soil without fertilizer seems to produce more blooms but less foliage. Aphids are the worst enemy of nasturtiums. Watch carefully for the first infestation and spray them immediately. Constant cutting encourages the growth of these plants.

I like the climbing varieties, which can be trained to astonishing heights on a trellis. The dwarf 'Golden Gleam' is attractive, and there are many varieties with new colors which are beautiful. Whether the flowers are double or single, the original *T. majus* or the newest hybrid pink, they are all attractive and flavorful.

Its Uses

Cut blossoms for salads, leaves and blossoms for sandwiches. Stuff flowers for canapes. Always wash the leaves and blossoms carefully to remove any residue of spray or stray aphids.

Orégano, *Origanum vulgare*

Oregano is a Eurasian plant, a member of the mint family; many varieties are attractive to grow. The leaves are fragrant, but most of them do not have the strong flavor of the dried product that comes from Greece, where it is native. At this writing I have a bag of blossoms and leaves from a hillside in Greece, and the odor is like that of the imported seasoning familiar to us. I have planted seeds of this and hope that they will germinate, because we need this good strong-flavored orégano.

The Plant

Oréganos available for culture are a white-flowered, somewhat hairy-leaved variety with a minty flavor and a very sweet smell when brushed or crushed; a small low-growing smooth-leafed type with bright-pink flowers, and an upright-stemmed small tender plant that resembles marjoram. The plant listed last is the one I use for seasoning.

It grows six to ten inches high.

Its Uses

Cut the top leaves to make the plant bush out, although any of the leaves can be used—in spaghetti, on pizza. Dried leaves can be used in tea mixtures. Use the blossoms and leaves of all oréganos in wreaths, swags, and bouquets both dried and green.

Parsley, *Petroselinum; P. crispum*, curled; *P. carum* or *apium*, plain-leafed or Italian

Parsley is native to Europe and grows wild in Sardinia. It has been cultivated in England since 1548. A Greek legend says the plant sprang from the blood of the hero Archemorus.

As a symbol, parsley has had many meanings: mirth, joy, festivity, honor, oblivion. The Greeks crowned their heroes with parsley wreaths and also used it to decorate tombs. They never used it in cooking. In Rome it stood for festivity. It was worn at banquets to prevent drunkenness, and was eaten during the meal and after it to remove the odor of foods heavily seasoned with garlic and onions. In this way it made its debut as a seasoning and garnish.

Stems of parsley were once dried and powdered for a dye. Parsley tea was prescribed for kidney disorders and, according to Turner, to cure sick fish in ponds.

The Plant

Parsley is a biennial, which means that it runs to seed in its second year. Be sure that the plants you buy or bring in from the garden are new growth. There are many varieties, but the common, or curly, kind and the Italian plain-leafed are best for indoor growing. Use at least six plants.

Pot the plants in a good garden soil and keep them in a cool, shaded place. (The shade of other plants will do.) Water them well and wash or syringe them frequently to improve their leafage. Cut the outside leaves for use, leaving the center to grow.

Parsley grows indoors from eight to ten inches high.

Its Uses

Do not think of parsley as just a garnish. Chop fresh green leaves and use them generously in soups, green salads, rice casseroles, and vegetable dishes. With tarragon and chives it makes a good *bouquet garni.*

Rosemary, *Rosmarinus officinalis*

Rosemary, most beautiful and fragrant of the seasoning herbs, is an evergreen from the Mediterranean area. It is used traditionally at weddings and funerals. It is the famous plant of memory, and stories of the Holy Family are told of it. As the first lady of the window garden, rosemary deserves the best of care and a place of prime importance. Use more than one.

The Plant

For an indoor garden two twelve-inch and two six-inch good terracotta pots are ideal. Never pin all your hopes on a single plant. Try more than one kind: *officinalis*, with narrow leaves and deep-blue blossoms; a gray-leafed one, less upright in growth, with softer leaves and lavender or pale-blue flowers, and the charming prostrate type with dark-green shining needle-like leaves and a woody stem that appears to be bonsai by nature. The prostrate rosemary creeps in all directions and has good deep-blue blossoms.

Rosemaries are most frequently brought in from the garden to winter. At this time one must remember that the plant has been growing steadily and enlarging its requirements. Although the root may not seem much bigger, the top certainly is. A generous amount of space is needed to keep the roots from becoming crowded, and sufficient soil for winter growth. Too often rosemaries, after a season outside, are put back in the same pots that housed them in their first year.

Although rosemaries are not overly susceptible, red spider mites may infect some of their leaves and not be visible or under control outdoors. Dry indoor heat aggravates the condition. Wash the underside of the leaves carefully when you remove them from the garden and spray them with a solution of malathion.

Make sure that the drainage holes in the pots are open because bottom drainage is essential. Water the plants from the top; spray the leaves at least once a week. It is difficult to do this in the house and that is one reason why rosemaries do well in a greenhouse, where the water spraying is likely to be daily routine.

Rosemaries like a cool growing place but do need light and some sun. I find that covering the top of the pots with sphagnum moss helps keep the roots from drying out. In most houses, rosemaries must be watered every day; they must never dry out. If the roots dry, no amount of water will restore them. Liquid fertilizer will help keep them in good growth, and a rich humus lightened with a little lime is the best potting medium.

As rosemaries grow relatively slowly indoors, they will not need much trimming; be careful not to cut into the woody stem because it is slow to recover. Plants that are freely watered and exposed to the heat of a house often make a pale false growth at the tips of the branches. It is best to cut this off down to the original growth, though often it dries out and disappears.

Indoors it grows from ten inches to three feet high.

Yellowing leaves may be due to too-tight potting, red spider mites, too much dry heat, insufficient light. Do not set the plants in a tub of water and leave them.

Rosemary seeds are slow in germinating; they need a whole season to develop, but it is interesting to grow plants from seed because unusual varieties often appear. If you buy the plants, examine them carefully for sturdy stems and good leaf color, remembering that there are both gray- and green-leaved varieties. A sturdy plant is a good buy and should grow into a fine specimen.

Its Uses

Clip leaves of rosemary to put into letters at Christmas time. Send small plants to friends as symbols of remembrance. Use them to season chicken and lamb, in punches and in jellies. Try the leaves to make tea. Tradition says that rosemary tea will restore mind and memory.

Sage, *Salvia officinalis*

Sage was once considered a cure-all for ills, particularly those related to old age. It was used as a wash to darken graying hair, teeth and gums were scrubbed with the leaves, and it was eaten in May by those who would "live for aye."

The Plant

Sage is a hardy plant outdoors and inside. It is sun- and lime-loving, likes some fertilizer, and needs good drainage. Indoors,

A grouping of various kinds of sage includes: above, the Mexican bush sage *Salvia leucantha;* to the right, Texas sage S. *coccinea;* and below, a planting of S. *officinalis* 'Tricolor'.

the thick pebbly leaves need frequent washing to prevent spider mites from disfiguring them.

Sage was one of the few herbs grown in my native Vermont and it was an important plant in the garden. In all the northern areas—Vermont, Maine, and eastern Canada—there was scarcely an attic or "woodshed chamber" that did not have bunches of sage hanging from the rafters, often in brown paper bags to protect them from dust. Sage tea was a common winter remedy and was always given to the aged, perhaps because the people knew that it was an Oriental symbol of immortality.

Sage was once thought to be an aid to digestion and its leaves, combined with parsley, were laid on banquet tables to be eaten to cut the fat in foods and to assist in digestion. It was natural that some bright cook should decide to place the sage in the cavity of birds and tuck it into a cut in roasts, thus originating stuffings.

It grows indoors from six to twelve inches high.

Its Uses

Green sage leaves are excellent in cheese dishes when used in moderation. Sage is also the principal seasoning in sausages, Vermont sage cheese, and most prepared stuffings. It is especially recommended for fatty meats.

Savory, winter and summer, *Satureja montana* and *S. hortensis*

The Plant

Summer savory, *hortensis,* is an annual plant native to Europe. It is the species most desirable as a seasoning, but winter savory, *montana,* a perennial, survives better indoors. Both like full sun, lime, and good drainage. They have many of the same properties, though winter savory grows like a small shrub. Summer savory can be grown from seeds but the seeds are slow in germinating.

It is better to use plants of both species.

Indoors savory is a sprawling plant, about eight inches high.

Its Uses

Cut small sprigs at any time for seasoning. Savory is especially good with string beans; with canned beans it takes away that unpleasant canned taste. It is also good in stuffings and herb mixtures where a piquant flavor is desired.

Sorrel, *Rumex scutatus*, French sorrel; *R. acetosa*, garden sorrel

The Plant

French sorrel is hardy in the garden but is well worth growing indoors because it produces such succulent leaves for a green soup and green meat sauces. Garden sorrel has much the same flavor but larger leaves. It is more readily available because it comes quickly from seeds.

The basal leaves are ovalish, arrow-shaped at the base, light-green in color, and about five inches long. The stem leaves narrow to a sharp point. If you like sorrel soup, plant four pots of it or one large container, with the plants embedded in deep rich soil. Deep pots are necessary because the plants have large roots and need adequate soil to produce good leaves. Keep the leaves cut back enough to prevent flowers and seeds from developing, otherwise the leaves become tough.

Sorrel needs plenty of water; it must never dry out. Water it every day—twice a day if the sun is hot. If it dries out accidentally, place the pot up to its rim in a basin of water and let it soak for an hour.

Check the underside of the leaves for mites. Curling leaves indicate their presence. Wash the leaves with a soap solution or plain water, using a force-spray.

The lax growth is about eight inches high.

Its Uses

Sorrel is used mainly in making soups, broths, and green sauces. Sauce for beef with chopped sorrel leaves is a favorite dish in Germanic countries.

Tarragon, *Artemisia dracunculus,* little dragon

Tarragon was once considered an antidote for the bites of mad dogs and the stings of insects and small dragons. There are two kinds. One, unfortunately, *can* be grown from seed which is offered for sale. Seeds produce a tall herbage which has no flavor when used in cooking. It is a native of northern Europe, Russia, and Siberia. Avoid using this seed outdoors or inside.

The Plant

True, or French, tarragon is a Mediterranean native and a hardy garden plant which is started from a root. The plant likes dryish, well-drained soil. If overwatered it often succumbs to root rot. Do not allow it to dry out, but be sure that the water has drained off before watering it again. Mature roots are large and it is better to pull small side starts from the main roots for indoor potting. A mature plant needs an eight- to ten-inch pot.

Tarragon needs sun to do its best, but will grow reasonably well in good light with sun for an hour or two a day. Indoors it seldom attains its maximum height of two feet, but will be about twelve to eighteen inches tall. Tarragon has few, if any, diseases and seldom needs attention other than water-spraying its leaves.

Its Uses

Cut green leaves from either top or side growth, always leaving about two inches of stem for future growth. The leaves have a slightly anise flavor. Tarragon is an excellent seasoning for fish, poultry, and steak, and is used in vinegars, salads, and herb mixtures—fine herbs particularly. It must be used sparingly, for its flavor is dominating. Dried tarragon has a very sweet odor; include it in some potpourris and in dried bouquets.

Thyme, *Thymus vulgaris*

There are many varieties of this charming little plant, among them the narrow-leafed French thyme, very gray in color, and the broad-leafed English thyme, low-growing and green. Thyme was once a symbol of bravery. It was one of the first plants used as incense. Mixed with juniper and rosemary, it was an important old-time disinfectant.

The Plant

Thymes are both creeping (*serpyllum*) and upright (*vulgaris*). Many are fragrant, but the most flavorsome are the French and English kinds, the lemon thymes, and *herba-barona,* caraway-scented thyme. All these plants like full sun, light limy soil, and excellent drainage. They are hardy indoors and out if given their requirements. Buy your plants for indoor growing.

Indoors thyme grows to various heights, but not more than ten inches.

Its Uses

Cut small sprigs at almost any time. This is a strong seasoning herb and should not be used with a heavy hand. Use it sparingly in soups, stuffings, and with pork and lamb. I always like it with roast lamb at Easter. Put a sprig in chowders. Add it to herb mixtures.

Water Cress, *Nasturtium officinale*

When nasturtium is mentioned in writings prior to the discovery of America, the reference is to water cress, not our flowering Indian cress. With the exception of parsley, there are few herbs that are more popular.

Water cress has been used from the earliest times as a green, a garnish, and as an antidote for scurvy. It makes a good salad to balance a heavy meal or to quicken the appetite. According to Nicholas Culpeper, the bruised leaves will cure facial blemishes.

The Plant

The flavor of water cress is similar to our flowering cress and the plants are closely related. The Latin name for both is derived from *nastus tortus,* convulsed nose, because of its pungency. The flowering plant, however, is now called *Tropaeolum.*

Few people feel that they can grow water cress without a running stream but I found, quite by accident, that it grows extremely well in cool parts of a moist greenhouse. I often empty packages of old seeds of doubtful germination in the very moist cutting bed and apparently I once included water cress seed because in a neglected spot toward the northwest, where there was little sun, great tendrils of it appeared. These established long roots and continued for several years. They blossomed and sowed seeds for new plants, which we potted in sphagnum moss, adding some light soil and lime. The seed also germinates in this medium.

A birdbath filled with this mixture will grow enough water cress for a small family. Place it in a shady part of the window garden and it will help keep your plantings moist. I use a terra-cotta birdbath about ten inches across. I fill it partially with wet sphagnum and sift a measuring cup of potting soil over the moss, filling the bath to within two inches of the rim. I then sprinkle the seeds on the surface, cover them with a little finely shredded moss, and fill the container with water. This is kept in the shade until green shoots pop through, when it can be given a little more light but not full sun. Cutting can start when the leaves are well formed. It is best to keep some seed sprouting; this can be done in a porous container.

It grows six to eight inches high, with long trailing tendrils.

Its Uses

Use as a salad green and as garnish.

4

Herbs to Grow for Fragrance

Fragrant plants have delighted man for centuries and perfumes have been made from them since the very dawn of history. Today we can buy a wide variety of rare or favorite perfumes in stores, but how much sweeter are the delicate scents of fresh flowers and aromatic leaves—outdoors or on a windowsill.

Many of the herbs that are grown indoors for their sweet odors exude their fragrance only when their leaves are bruised or brushed. Sun and water release the fragrance of others.

Among the best-loved house plants for scent are the geraniums, but there are many others.

The lovely calamondin, a miniature orange tree with tiny fruits, will fill a room with June-bride sweetness when it blooms. Other plants that can be grown indoors are jasmine, sweet-olive, and heliotrope with white or purple flowers. Some of these plants also have culinary uses.

Cardamom, *Elettaria cardamomum*

Cardamom is a very handsome foliage plant of the ginger family, excellent for a shady spot. It has long dark-green sharply tapered leaves that emit a spicy odor when brushed.

I have never seen this plant in bloom and cannot recommend it as a source of cardamom seeds, but its healthy green color and sweet scent make it a desirable addition to the window garden.

It often reaches an indoor height of three feet in an old plant.

Costmary, *Chrysanthemum balsamita*, Bible leaf, sweet Mary, alecost

A native of the Orient, costmary was popular in Western gardens from the sixteenth through the eighteenth century. In colonial America its leaves were used as markers in Bibles and prayer books; hence the name Bible leaf. Used in ale, it imparted a mint flavor and was considered a curative for "disorders of the stomach and head."

Costmary resembles tansy in its flowering top, but its leaves, instead of being fernlike, are long, broad, and tapered, with finely toothed margins. In outdoor gardens the plant reaches a height of two to four feet. In pot cultivation it is seldom more

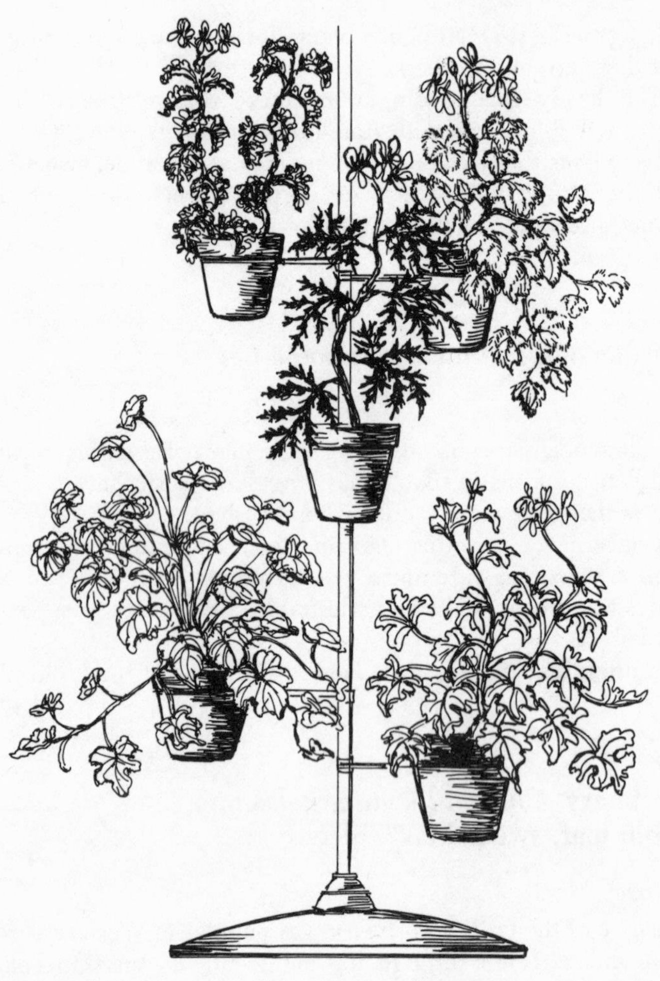

A geranium "tree" displays: above left, the lemon-scented *Pelargonium crispum* 'Prince Rupert'; above right, the peppermint *P. tomentosum;* center, *P. radans* 'Skeleton Rose'; below left, apple-scented *P. odoratissimum;* and below right, the spicy, nutmeg-scented *P. fragrans.*

than eighteen inches tall unless placed in a large container. It likes sun, well-drained soil, and an ample amount of water.

Indoors it grows from twelve to eighteen inches high.

Its Uses

In southern Europe a leaf is sometimes used in omelets and scrambled eggs, but the minty flavor is an acquired taste. A conserve has been made from its flowers. Grow it for its clean mintlike odor and for its association with the household practices of an earlier day when costmary and lavender were used together to scent linens and clothing. I still use it in this way.

Geranium, *Pelargonium*, garden geranium, stork's-bill geranium

Few plants dispense as much fragrance as the scented geraniums. Just brushing their foliage causes them to exude their sweet and varied odors. They are natives of the Cape of Good Hope, where they grow tree-tall. In all, there are about two hundred and fifty species; of these fifty to seventy-five are worth cultivating.

Do not collect these plants for their blooms, which are small and insignificant, but for their scented foliage. The collection and culture of scented geraniums could fill a lifetime. Those in my plant window were selected for fragrance and flavor and to add leaf interest to my indoor garden. Only a few kinds can be described here, but the enthusiast who is successful in growing them will soon find many others to add to his collection.

Care of Geraniums

Given proper care, good *Pelargonium* plants will last for many years. Rule one is to give them ample space and sun for at least part of the day.

Watering

Geraniums should not be overwatered and should never stand in water. I personally do not believe in allowing them to reach the wilting point before watering them, as is sometimes recommended. If the plants become too dry, their leaves are likely to lose their good appearance.

Watering once a day in the warm atmosphere of the modern home is not too much. Every other day will do if the temperature is fifty to sixty and the potting is adequate. On sunless days or in poor light another day might go by without damage to the plants. Keeping them on the dry side has, in my opinion, often been misinterpreted, to the ruination of many plants. To me, the phrase means keeping them on the *well-drained* side. Make sure that the plants are taking up the water you apply and that the pots are not holding a residue. If there is a residue, skip a day. The best time to water geraniums is in the morning before eleven, or at that time.

Trimming

All pelargoniums need frequent trimming. The customary advice is to cut them back, and the usual question is, "To what point?" This naturally depends upon the time of year and the condition of the plants. Pinch out the rapidly growing tops of young plants, leaving the lower growth and stems. This makes a better-shaped plant.

Fertilizing

To fertilize geraniums, water them every two weeks with a weak solution of Rapid Gro or similar product. (Do not use dry plant foods; they are not easily assimilated in the home.) Syringe the foliage and allow the water-soluble fertilizer to go into the pot.

Insects

Check the plants at least once a month for aphids, white fly, or red spider mites. If there is an infestation spray them with an insecticide, Black Leaf 40 or malathion.

Rose Geranium, *P. graveolens,* sweet rose

Of all scented geraniums, the old-fashioned sweet rose is the all-time favorite. If you want an authentic specimen—the kind Grandma used in jelly—choose your plant carefully. *Graveolens* has a woody stem, rounded five- to seven-lobed very fragrant leaves, and rose-pink flowers. Leaves of this geranium and of the skeleton-leafed geranium are used in flavoring.

Its Uses

Add them to jelly. A leaf in warm water, syrup, or sugar will impart a roselike flavor. Use dried leaves in a potpourri mixture and in tea. Line a cake tin with leaves for a rose-geranium cake. Make geranium biscuits.

There are other geraniums that resemble sweet rose at certain stages but are not suitable for culinary use. They have varied fragrances, however, and are well worth growing in a window garden. Among them are 'Pungent Rose', with a larger leaf; 'Little Gem', a charming small-leafed rose variety of compact growth; 'Lady Plymouth', with variegated green and white foliage; 'Gray Lady Plymouth', with grayish-green leaves, and 'Mint Rose', with a white band on the leaves and a strong mint odor mingled pleasantly with its rose scent.

Lemon Rose, *P. graveolens* 'Rober's Rose'

In my opinion 'Rober's Rose' has the sweetest of all the rose scents in the *graveolens* group. Its growth is not as attractive as the others—it resembles a tomato plant—but its odor is superlative. Its thicker leaves are tempting to insects, so be on guard.

Skeleton Rose, *P. graveolens* 'Dr. Livingstone'

Indoors and out, this is one of my greatest favorites. Its odor reminds me of a hot summer day when all the scents of the garden come together. It is like a rose sachet mixture or the essence of rose geranium, but sweeter.

I keep a dried bouquet of its leaves on my desk when I write in winter. Touching them is like a visit to a summer garden. I always bring in bunches of the rose types to hang by our fireplaces. Curious visitors finger the leaves with wonder and when they crush them are surprised to find that an entirely different plant can smell so much like roses. The uses of this geranium in cooking are the same as those given for sweet rose.

Apple Geranium, *P. odoratissimum*

The apple geranium has small rounded leaves, light green in color, finely but not deeply serrated. The leaves become larger as the plant matures, and velvety in texture. The plant expands from the crown but does not grow tall and therefore does not need to be pinched back like most varieties. The odor is like that of winter apples. In fact, the plant never fails to remind me of the apple barrel that was kept in the cellar of my Vermont home during winter.

Attar of Roses, *P. graveolens* 'Attar of Roses'

This variety is often sought out because the name has such a pleasant connotation. Personally, I prefer 'Dr. Livingstone' or 'Rober's Rose', but this plant is part of a rose collection and has many admirers.

Lemon Geranium, *P. crispum*

All of the lemon-scented geraniums are fascinating to grow, but in a limited space we must confine our enthusiasm to those that have the greatest number of herbal uses. For this reason I reject 'Prince Rupert' varieties, as attractive as they are, and concentrate on *P. crispum.*

It is a vigorous grower, an excellent plant for a large tub or pot, and it is the most fragrant of the larger-growing lemon geraniums. I also suggest the variety *P. crispum minor*, often called the finger-bowl geranium.

Its Uses

The dried leaves are good for potpourris and dried bouquets. I use them in tea and punch and as a garnish for lemon desserts.

Nutmeg Geranium, *P. fragrans*

The nutmeg geranium has fan-shaped leaves, crenated and toothed, although both these characteristics vary. The foliage is very gray and soft, and the plant has a trailing tendency that recommends it for hanging baskets and the ends of planters, where it will spill over the side. Its odor is sweet and spicy.

Like the apple geranium, the nutmeg variety is primarily for beauty. They are sometimes included in potpourris and dried-flower arrangements.

Peppermint Geranium, *P. tomentosum*

The dainty fragrance of the mint geranium was familiar in our grandmothers' day and the plant must have filled many a bay window in the past. It is a trailing plant that grows quickly as a bedding plant in the garden. In a kettle or tub it will adequately cover the ground and spill over the sides. This poses difficulties in housing them for the winter. Unless they are cut back drastically, they will die. Many growers prefer to use small well-rooted cuttings in indoor gardens. Start them in two-inch pots and transfer them to four- or six-inch pots as they develop. They are very attractive in a hanging basket.

Its Uses

The great heart-shaped leaves are decorative in flower arrangements and interesting as a garnish for mint desserts. I have often surrounded a gelatin salad with them. The leaves press well and are interesting in plant pictures with pressed flowers, and against the glass in rose jars. They also make good bookmarks.*

Heliotrope, *Heliotropium peruvianum*, cherry pie

The heliotropes are natives of South America, and Peru has given her name to *Heliotropium peruvianum* which has vanilla-scented flowers. Cherry pie was a favorite Victorian scent. Along with violets, it was popular in my generation for Easter Sunday nosegays, and I recall it pleasantly as my mother's favorite perfume. Heliotrope sachets and toilet waters were popular scents a generation ago and the odor takes one back through the years.

Heliotrope came from Peru in 1757 and became popular in both America and England. English gardeners made standards of it in the fashion of that day, and this art is being practiced again in twentieth-century gardens. The Harkness Gardens, near New London, Connecticut, are famous for their magnificent heliotrope trees.

A small tree is excellent for a window garden. To produce it, persistently clip side shoots as they appear, and apply a good fertilizer. The potting soil should be rich but well drained.

* For those who are interested in a more comprehensive study of geraniums in their many aspects, I suggest Helen Van Pelt Wilson's *Joy of Geraniums* as the most complete book on the subject. For a brief account of the scented geraniums, my booklet *Caprilands Grandmother's Geraniums* is available.

Standards need the support of a firm stake. Their tops should be kept trimmed and their flowers should be pinched off until a firm standard or trunk, say three to five feet high, is formed. This requires patience and persistence and about four years of growing.

Jasmine, *Jasminum*

There are about two hundred jasmine species, all native to Persia, India, and warm countries of the Old World. Only a few are available for house cultivation.

In India jasmine is held sacred to Vishnu and is used as a votive offering in religious ceremonies. Flowers are made into garlands for distinguished guests.

White jasmine, *J. officinale*, is a shrub native to nothern India and Persia. It was brought to Europe in the sixteenth century. In southern Europe it is thoroughly acclimatized; in the northern part it must be grown indoors. Outdoors it blooms from June to October; inside it blooms all winter. The leaves are dark green, opposite, and pinnate. The flowers come on the young shoots, so use care in pruning. They are funnel-shaped, white, and very fragrant. Usually a few open at a time. My plant scrambles over the window and does not seem to mind the cold glass.

J. grandiflorum is from the Himalayas, though it is often called Spanish jasmine. It resembles *officinale* but its branches are shorter and stronger and the flowers are larger and reddish underneath. This is the species most highly prized by perfumers. (Cape jasmine, *Gardenia jasminoides*, is the gardenia of florists.)

Jasmine grows to an average of two feet indoors, and may get to five or six feet when very old.

Its Uses

Grow jasmines as ornaments and for their fragrance. Flowers can be added to tea. Make jasmine water with fresh flowers. Try jasmine sugar.

Lavender, *Lavandula vera*, true lavender

Lavender, one of the world's best-loved plants, is so associated with the English countryside that it is difficult to realize that it came to Britain as an immigrant. It was introduced around 1568. It was widely planted and greatly cherished so that the plant and its scent became identified with England.

Lavender is a perennial plant, indigenous to the Mediterranean area from the Canary Islands to India. It was known in Africa, northern Arabia, and the Holy Land, and is probably one of the nards mentioned in the Bible from which the anointing oil spikenard was derived.

It was a tradition in Spain and Portugal to strew the floors of homes and public places with lavender for the sweet fragrance it yields when trodden on. In England, lavender was burned with thyme in the St. John's Eve fires to drive away evil spirits. As an antiseptic and an ingredient of the famous four-thieves vinegar, it invaded the realm of English medicine. Arabian physicians had used it in this way for generations.

Lavender conserves were made and used to "comfort the stomach" and dried flowers were worn on the heads of farmers in hayfields to avert sunstroke. Spirits of lavender were used for giddiness and faintness, to raise the spirits, and to promote the appetite. In the form of an oil, lavender was combined with rosemary, cinnamon bark, nutmeg, red sandalwood, and wine to make the well-known lavender drops known as "red lavender" or "palsy drops."

Lavender was also used to preserve virtue. We associate it with soaps, powders, toilet waters, and sachets.

In the indoor garden, lavender often flowers in the spring but not as profusely as it does outdoors, especially in its first year. But even if bloom is sparse, the gray leaves dispense a fragrance that makes the winter-weary think of spring.

Culture

Lavender requires well-drained sandy or gravelly soil and a dry atmosphere. It needs sun to be at its best, but it does well if it gets good light. A few blossoms will come on one-year-old plants, maximum bloom in the third year. Give the plants air and space; otherwise the leaves will blacken. Remove any such leaves. New leaves will come when growing conditions are rectified.

Species to Grow

For indoor growing, I especially like four species which I shall now describe, though others will grow well in a window garden.

Fern-leafed lavender, *L. abrontonoides*

Fern-leafed lavender is of graceful growth, with greenish-gray foliage that is more pungent than sweet. The plant grows to two feet indoors. Its blooms are its chief charm, but its interesting leaf structure, rapid growth, and adaptability to pot culture all recommend it. I have found that it self-sows abundantly and that the tiny fernlike seedlings that come up develop very quickly into flowering plants. It blooms constantly if it is kept in a sunny window.

Toothed lavender, *L. dentata*

Toothed lavender is of interesting growth and has attractive gray or green leaves, sharply indented. The deep-purple or lavender flowers, on short stems, are without fragrance, but the leaves are scented. *Dentata* becomes a small shrub outdoors but inside it is easily contained in a four- to six-inch pot. Its decorative leaves are effective in flower arrangements and nosegays.

It grows from twelve to twenty-four inches high indoors.

L. stoechas

L. stoechas is of such great historical interest that no collection should be without it. It can become a shrub growing to three feet, but usually in Connecticut grows less than half that tall. The leaves are gray, densely hairy and lance-shaped. The dark-purple blossoms are crowded on a thick spike. This species is grown for its flowers; it is not highly scented.

L. heterophylla

Heterophylla has been a favorite plant at Caprilands for many years. Its name refers to the different kinds of leaves that grow on the same plant. They are blue-gray, thick, and aromatic. Just brushing them releases their fragrance. Dried, they fill a room with the scent of sweet grass and new-mown hay. The blossoms come on long spikes and have little color. This lavender grows large in the garden; indoors it requires a six- to ten-inch pot to hold the summer's growth. *Heterophylla* is for fragrance and decorations.

It reaches a height indoors of one to two feet, or more on older plants.

Uses of Lavender

Lavender toilet water can be made at home and, with vinegar, is a soothing preparation for headaches. I burn bits of discarded leaves and blossoms as incense and use dried leaves in sachets. Other uses include a tea made of leaves and blossoms, a garnish for summer drinks (blossoms), lavender jelly made with the flowers and apple juice, and lavender sugar made like vanilla sugar. Lavender is also an insect repellent. In a foot bath it soothes aching feet.

Lemon Balm, *Melissa officinalis*

Lemon balm was once believed to be of great benefit to the nervous system. From early Greek and Roman times up to the Victorian era, it was given for all types of nervous disorders. John Evelyn wrote, "Balm is soverrign for the brain, strengthening the memory and powerfully chasing away melancholy." *Melissa* means "bee" in Greek, and the name was given to this plant because it attracts bees. Hives were rubbed with it to bring in swarms.

While lemon balm grows to two or more feet outdoors, it will stay within a foot inside. Its leaves are crinkled and its growth most attractive if it is cut back frequently. The blossoms are insignificant.

This plant grows easily from seed, but the seeds are slow in germinating. Two good small plants should yield all the cut leaves that the average home can use. Keep the blossoms cut off because the plant is more attractive before it blooms. Balm is a mint and like other mints will grow in either sun or shade.

Its Uses

When the plant has attained a height of three or four inches, cut leaves from the top and use them in drinks and wine. Dried, they can be used to make tea. This is one of the sweetest smelling of all the herbs and is a good ingredient for a potpourri. It is also attractive in household bouquets. Just to brush it in passing is a pleasure.

Lemon Verbena, *Lippia citriodora*, herba Louisa and *Aloysia citriodora* in South America

Lemon verbena is a deciduous shrub native to Chile, Peru, and the Guatemalan highlands. It grows to apple-tree height in the

An epergne holds a collection of fruit-scented herbs—at the top, lemon verbena *Lippia citriodora,* with orange mint *Mentha citrata* alongside; in the center, lemon geraniums *Pelargonium crispum;* below, plants of lemon thyme *Thymus serpyllum vulgaris.*

shadow of volcanoes, where its long glossy yellow-green leaves give off the most ravishing lemon odor known to man. It was taken to Europe by the *conquistadores* and reached England in the latter part of the eighteenth century. It was known in our Southern states in 1800.

In its native countries lemon verbena is used medicinally for stomach disorders and as a skin stimulant. Its leaves are also used for a popular tea and were once considered a substitute for China tea.

Lemon verbena should be brought in from the New England garden in October. It grows too large to winter in an average-size window, reaching a height of three to six feet. It can be cut back severely, but if you wish to have tall, handsome trees, winter it in the basement near a window or give it a place in the indoor garden where it can be surrounded by other more attractive winter plants.

This shrub bitterly resents our seasonal changes and drops its leaves as soon as it is potted. Save them because they make a wonderful sachet and a good tea. Give the plant some light and keep it well watered. It does not need sun and will do well in a cool spot but don't let it freeze. Usually after January small bits of green leaves will form along the nodes where branches will come later. If the room is warm, they may develop into full leaves; often they will drop several times before the final leaves form. Flowers come in July and August—small, purple, and of little interest.

Do not depend upon verbenas for a window display; but suffer with them, for when they come to life after their winter rest they are priceless. Small plants often keep their leaves through much of the winter, however. If they are kept free of their worst enemy, the red spider mite, they will add to the window's beauty.

Its Uses

Try the freshly dried leaves in a tea, but *do* brew it for at least ten minutes, because they yield their flavor slowly. Use dried leaves for potpourris when they have matured.

Mint, *Mentha*

All mints came originally from the Mediterranean area, although many have become naturalized in other places and are often classified with native plants. They were introduced into England by the Romans and were brought to America by the colonists. Mint is important in medieval lists of plants. It was cultivated in monastery gardens and used by herbalist physicians for such assorted ailments as watering of the eyes, headaches, failing memory, sore mouth and gums, and dandruff. Culpeper advised that "rose leaves petals and mint, heated and applied outwardly, cause rest and sleep." The dandies of ancient civilizations used mints in their bath water.

Culpeper wrote, in *Plants of Wisdom,* "The smelle rejoiceth the heart of man, for which cause they used to strew it in chambers and places of recreation, pleasure and repose, where feasts and banquets are made."

Mints were named for Menthe, a nymph loved by Pluto, god of the underworld. When Persephone discovered his attachment for her, her jealousy was aroused and she transformed Menthe into a plant—a plant that would forever seek underground waters and shady places, looking for her lost god.

Apple Mint, *M. rotundifolia*

Apple mint has rough gray-green rounded leaves with a mint-apple odor. Grown in a large pot or tub, it will stay within bounds indoors, growing one to two feet high or spreading and trailing; outdoors it spreads rapidly and needs a great deal of room.

Its Uses

This is a particularly good species for tea. I dry quantities of it for our special Caprilands tea mixture. The leaves are excellent for candying, decorative in floral arrangements, and good for general seasoning purposes.

Corsican Mint, *M. requienii,* baby's-tears

Corsican mint is a small creeping plant with such tiny leaves that it looks like moss. A touch releases its odor, however, and identifies it as a mint.

Grow Corsican mint in wet sand. In one of our greenhouses it jumped out of the spot planned for it into the sand which covers the floor and grew luxuriantly under a propagating bench. Small plants, in a mixture of sand and vermiculite similar to that under the bench, spread rapidly over the edges of their pots and make a fragrant border. Sink a small pot of it in a wet propagating mixture and keep it moist. Like its namesake, Menthe, it seeks shade or murky light and is at a disadvantage in the sun.

Indoors it grows flat and hardly an inch high.

Its Uses

Corsican mint is for fragrance. It is said that in the past it flavored the cordial crème de menthe, but I find little proof of this. Enjoy it as an interesting plant; use the leaves and tiny blooms in miniature garden scenes and flower arrangements.

Orange Mint, *M. citrata*

Citrata has an odor that is sweet beyond belief, a combination of the scents of orange, bergamot, and sweet basil. It has a dark stem and rounded deep-green leaves, purple underneath—one of the most attractive herbs you could have in your indoor garden.

It reaches a height of six to eight inches.

Its Uses

Use the leaves in punch with orange juice, and as a tea. It is excellent in a potpourri.

Peppermint, *M. piperita*

The peppermint species is very decorative. I prefer and grow the English black peppermint, which has dark stems and leaves with a purplish cast. The blooms are attractive, in color dark purple.

It grows six to twelve inches high indoors.

Its Uses

Use the leaves to make peppermint tea, and for fragrance in bouquets.

Pineapple Mint, *M. variegata*

Pineapple mint is a highly decorative plant with leaves variegated with white and cream. Their odor is more like pineapple than mint. Grown indoors, it is apt to be trailing and thus is suitable for a hanging basket or the edge of a window box.

Its Uses

Cut branches for bouquets, use it as a garnish, add a leaf to a cup of tea.

Spearmint, *M. spicata*

Spearmint, named for its pointed leaves, is the most popular of the mints and the one most often used for flavoring. There are several mints with a similar taste, but the best for all purposes is *spicata*.

Grow spearmint from roots, not from seed. One root, well started, will multiply fast and supply all your needs. This plant has no special preference as to soil, grows in either sun or shade, and benefits from frequent cutting.

Indoors it grows to twelve inches.

Its Uses

Cut the leaves for use in mint sauce, pea soup, tea, jellies, and salads.

Myrtle, *Myrtus communis*, and *M. communis microphylla*, true myrtle

True myrtle is a shrub or tree native to western Asia. A common tree in the Holy Land, it was once used with other greens at the Feast of the Tabernacles as a symbol of the highest good. There is an old Hebrew saying, "Those that are just are compared to myrtles."

Myrtle was once used with bay, or in place of it, for wreaths conferred on poets, priests, and other distinguished citizens. In this role it symbolized love and immortality. In the Bible it often signified peace and joy. The Greeks and Romans, however, dedicated it to the Goddess of Love as a symbol of passion. Myrtle trees surrounded Greek temples in ancient times and are being planted around them today in various restorations.

There are two possible sources of the name *Myrtus*. It could refer to Myrtilus, son of Mercury, who betrayed his master and was transformed into a myrtle tree when the sea rejected his body. Or it could have been named for the nymph Myrene, who dared to love a human and was turned into a myrtle by the angry goddess Venus.

Myrtle groves are often used in Italian paintings as a background for the figure of the Goddess of Love, because legend says that Venus and her nymphs, when surprised by satyrs, found refuge in a thick grove of myrtle.

There are many varieties of the true myrtle but the one most prized is *microphylla*, thickly branched, with very small dark-green leaves that look as if they had been polished. Its flowers are charming, small and white with raylike centers. *Microphylla* has been cultivated for centuries in the Western world as a symbol of love.

Brides in Sweden and other northern countries wear it as a wedding crown and in England a sprig of it is included with rosemary in the bride's bouquet. With rue, it is a symbol of virginity in Lithuania and Poland, and sprigs of it were pinned on the bridal gown, around the hem, and in the veil and bodice.

Culture

Myrtle is one of the best of the house plants. It does well in sun or shade and grows slowly the first year. It can be trained into bonsai form or clipped to make a handsome topiary tree. Few, if any, insects attack it and it needs little attention—just a change of pots as it grows and much watering. Do not ever let it dry out.

The average plant when purchased is six to eight inches high and should do well in a three- to four-inch pot. Several years will pass before it needs more space. Old myrtles require ten- to fourteen-inch pots or tubs. It may eventually reach a height of five feet.

Its Uses

Commercially, the flowers, fruit, and bark of the myrtle tree are used in perfumes, and the bark and roots are also used for tanning the best Russian leather. In the home, its uses are sentimental and decorative. A sprig can be cut for a Valentine gift because myrtle is a symbol of love, or it can be used in a bouquet. I make a crown of these tiny leaves to garnish our spring-lamb cake, and crowns for Valentine cupids. I also use myrtle in spirals and garlands for Christmas candlesticks.

Orange Tree, *Citrus mitis*, calamondin

It is hard to imagine what my plant window would be like without my little orange trees. Through December and January, the air has been sweet with the scent of orange blossoms. For Christmas I placed one on each side of an Italian statue of the Virgin and Child at the end of the long living room. The terracotta pots which held them and the colors of their fruit and foliage toned with a halo of Della Robbia fruits above the Virgin's head. The arrangement was appropriate because the orange is one of the plants dedicated to the Virgin Mary. It symbolizes purity, chastity, and generosity.

Culture

Citrus mitis grows to a height of about two feet when potted. It is upright in habit, has glossy bright-green leaves, white fragrant blossoms, and one-inch orangelike fruits. Sometimes it bears fruits and flowers at the same time. I always plant orange trees in terracotta pots and give them little attention except to apply fertilizer and occasionally add some fresh soil.

Its Uses

Orange trees are primarily for fragrance and decoration. The fruits are bitter and acid, but L. H. Bailey says that the juice is well flavored and that among ade-making fruits it is unsurpassed. I have made marmalade with them and preserved them whole in syrup like kumquats, with rum or brandy added. They are excellent.

Pineapple Sage, *Salvia rutilans*

Pineapple sage is a stunning herb from Mexico, tender and with a scent like pineapple. Outdoors it grows very fast and becomes a giant in one season. Indoors, it can be confined in a six- to eleven-inch pot, although it will attain its full height in a tub. If a plant is purchased, it will probably be a small one. Cut it back if it grows too fast to keep it window-size. The blossoms, which come in late fall and early winter, are a brilliant red and are arranged on spikes. If young plants are used they will bloom in winter. After flowering, the plant can be cut back to the crown leaves and allowed to grow again.

It grows twelve to eighteen inches high indoors, and larger in tubs if it is not trimmed back.

Some sun is a requirement of pineapple sage, but an hour a day will bring it into blossom. In good light, without sun, the plant will remain green and fragrant. Pineapple sage is extremely tender and must be kept away from a freezing window. If you bring it in from the garden, spray it before placing it with other plants. It will need checking for red spider mites and white fly at least twice during the season indoors.

Its Uses

Grow pineapple sage for fragrance; it has very little flavor. It is an excellent garnish, however. Its light-green leaves are decorative and its odor in association with food is delightful. Try it around a gelatin salad that contains pineapple fruit. Cut garnish leaves from the side, leaving the center spike intact for blossoming.

Sweet-Olive, *Osmanthus fragrans*

Sweet-olive is a shrub with tiny, white, very fragrant flowers during winter. It has been a greenhouse favorite of mine for years. Its native home is Asia, where it grows to thirty feet. Old greenhouse plants develop a trunk like a tree and grow to the roof. In the window culture it is quite possible to keep its maximum to a ten-inch pot, while a starting plant will be quite comfortable in a four- to six-inch container.

It reaches an indoor height of about two feet.

The plant is undemanding as to light and culture. It blossoms in good light and the blooms last longer if it is not in full sun. The flowers are inconspicuous but their fragrance will scent a room. Grow sweet-olive with your fragrant herbs and, if possible, put it in an outdoor garden in the spring.

Its Uses

This little tree is for decoration and fragrance only.

Thyme, *Thymus*

The fragrance of some of the thymes recommends them for inclusion in the fragrant group of herbs. French thyme belongs here as well as in the flavoring section, where it is more fully described.

Caprilands Thyme

I call this sweet-smelling plant Caprilands because it has not been otherwise identified. It thrives under the conditions described for caraway-thyme but has a pleasant trailing habit. The leaves are small and their color varies somewhat with the soil and exposure to the sun but tend to be a grayish green.

Outdoors, it is hardy and will completely cover a wall. Indoors, it trails over the edges of pots, window boxes and hanging containers. Its odor is like a garden of May flowers, a blend of many fragrances with a suggestion of spice.

Its Uses

Grow it for its attractive scent and as an ornament. It has little flavor.

Caraway Thyme, *T. herba-barona*

Caraway thyme earned its name in the days when it was used to cure a baron of beef, a sirloin cut. In the years before re-

Large wicker breadbaskets suspended by chains (heavy cord could be used) from window casings make attractive containers for a collection of thymes. Above, the lemon *Thymus serpyllum vulgaris* and silver *T. s. argenteus;* below, mother-of-thyme *T. serpyllum*, golden lemon thyme *T. s. aureus*, and caraway thyme *T. herba-barona*.

frigeration, thyme was used to prevent spoilage and to add flavor to meats.

This plant grows in a wire mound of delicate stems with small glossy leaves. It responds happily to indoor cultivation. Pot it in a shallow pot or dish, in soil which is partly sand and gravel. I have successfully used a small flat with its usual good drainage, putting small stones in the bottom and a mixture of gravelly soil from the garden, plus a four-ounce-pot measure of good potting soil and teaspoonful of lime. It will grow in a much richer medium but does not then retain its strong caraway scent.

Indoors it grows four inches high.

Its Uses

While caraway thyme is grown for fragrance, the leaves can be used for seasoning. Cut them anywhere; new ones will appear.

French Thyme, *T. vulgaris,* narrow-leafed gray or green thyme

French thyme is a small shrub with a woody stem and upright needlelike leaves. So redolent are the leaves with the sweet but stimulating thyme scent that Kipling called it "dawn in paradise."

Outdoors, it grows best in well-limed soil and full sun. Indoors, it needs a somewhat large pot because its numerous roots must be kept well covered. Fill the pot with potting soil and add two teaspoonfuls of lime. The plants need three or four hours of sun daily for proper growth.

It will reach a height of eight to ten inches indoors.

Its Uses

Grow French thyme for fragrance and flavor. Its culinary uses are described in the chapter on flavoring herbs.

Lemon thyme, *T. citriodorus, T. serpyllum vulgaris, T. serpyllum aureus*

Lemon thymes are among the most fragrant plants in the world. When brushed they give off a ravishing sweet-lemon odor. Gold-leaf lemon is usually referred to as golden thyme, but this name is confusing because there is another golden thyme that has no lemon scent.

Aureus is a low growing, almost creeping plant that will trail over the edge of a pot most attractively. *Vulgaris*, bush lemon, is somewhat shrubby, with plain green leaves.

Citriodorus is bushlike and has light-green leaves with golden edges.

The odor of the lemon thymes reminds us that they were once called incense plants and were used alone or in combination with other dried herbs as fumigants.

For the window garden any or all of these charmers would be desirable. They need a maximum of sun and do best in a southern window. They enjoy dry conditions but must not be allowed to dry out to the roots.

Its Uses

Use the leaves for a tea or in potpourris, or just enjoy their beauty and fragrance.

Woodruff, *Asperula odorata*, waldmeister, Whitsunday herb

Woodruff is a charming plant of the madder family that dispenses its fascinating fragrance only when dried. An old song by an unknown author sings its praise:

The woodruff is a bonny flower, her leaves are set like spurs
About her stem and honey-sweet is every flower of hers.
Yet sweetest dried and laid aside in kist with linen white
Or hung in bunches from the roof for wintry delight.
The woodruff is a bonny flower. We press her into wine
To make a cordial comfort for sickly folk that pine.
We plant our graves with woodruff, and still on holy days
Woodruff on country altars gives out her scent of praise.

Woodruff was not used in wine *only* for medicinal purposes. It is the chief ingredient of the famous May wine served at Caprilands at our opening festivities. In Germany it seasons the *maitrank* and in many parts of central Europe it is happily combined with champagne or brandy. At Caprilands, strawberries always decorate the bowl and are used in profusion to flavor and color the wine.

Outdoors, woodruff is a ground cover for acid soil in the shade—under trees and on banks. It sends out runners which produce new plants. In the window garden, a number of plants can be used together in a shallow planter with drainage holes. Though woodruff thrives in the shade, it must have drainage to survive.

My best planting of woodruff is in combination with ivies in a western window which affords light but no sun. The container is a painted metal tray covered with sphagnum moss. Into this medium roots of ivy were forced and the resulting plants have been growing for four years. After the Christmas holidays, the ivies are fertilized and sprayed and the whole tray is soaked. The leaves are washed on both sides, new sphagnum and liquid fertilizer are added, and as much good new soil as the tray will hold.

The woodruff plants are then added so that they will be ready for spring parties. Small potted plants are used. The ball of soil from the two-inch pot is forced into the sphagnum, a spoonful of earth is added, and the plant is on its way to the May celebration. But have enough plants to leave some uncut. Those left will blossom in late April or early May with white starlike flowers.

Its Uses

When the plant is three or four inches high, cut it back to its roots and dry it. Add it to white wine, Rhine, Reisling, or dry Sauterne. Let it remain in the wine for several days, or at least overnight. The resulting beverage is beyond compare. Woodruff also makes a good jelly and a sweet glaze for chicken or venison. The scent of dried woodruff has been described as a blend of the sweet odors of new-mown hay, sweet grass, and peach blossoms.

5

Herbs to Grow for Fun

Some herbs are interesting to grow in a winter window garden though they have no culinary or medicinal uses and are not distinctively fragrant. They add interesting forms, foliage, or flowers to the collection and have legendary powers which are fascinating to recall.

Often in an outdoor garden the individuality of these plants goes unnoticed among showier species. Indoors we turn the spotlight on them and learn to know them intimately.

I call these herbs plants for fun. Again the category is loose because some have occasional uses. And of course all herbs are fun to those who love them.

Angelica, *Angelica archangelica, A. officinalis*

An entire book could be written about angelica, so steeped is this herb in folklore. It was used as a protection against infection. It was kept over winter in the far north and the stems were eaten as greens to prevent scurvy. In parts of northern Germany and in Lapland it was the custom to carry flowering branches of angelica in processions to the accompaniment of a chant in a tongue so ancient that few could interpret it. These practices date to a pre-Christian era.

Christian teaching changed, but did not destroy, these festivals; they were merely given a Christian interpretation. Legend says that an angel appeared in the time of a great plague and brought angelica as a cure. It was also said that because it blossoms on the day of the archangel St. Michael it provided powerful protection against all evil spells. Thus it earned the name "root of the Holy Ghost."

Culture

Angelica likes a moist fairly rich soil and shade. It is a biennial that blossoms, sows its seeds, and dies.

As the plant grows it needs frequent changing to larger pots. It reaches a height of five feet out of doors. It seldom blooms indoors, although in a larger container it could bloom in its second year. But given good soil, plenty of moisture, and an adequate container, it should produce interesting leaves and some stems for candying.

It will grow twelve to twenty-four inches high indoors.

Its Uses

Angelica leaves have the taste and smell of juniper and are good in drinks and in jellies. The stems can be candied for use on cakes and cookies. It takes a lot of angelica to make candying worth while because the process is long and involved. I suggest growing this plant just for fun.

Artemisia, *Artemisia abrotanum*, southernwood; *A. camphorata*, camphor-scented

Artemisias are often included in fragrance gardens, notably as border plants. They produce masses of delicate dill-like foliage, but only a few dispense pleasant odors.

"Old man" and "lad's-love," names given this plant in the past, suggest some of its uses. "Old man" refers to the gray-green foliage of *abrotanum* and the symbolic planting on the right of the front door to indicate the old man of the house. On the left was planted a low-growing, very gray artemisia, possibly *A. pontica* or *A. stelleriana,* which was called the "old woman." This planting was an English tradition, followed by early colonists.

The name "lad's-love" has several possible sources. Sprays of southernwood were included in the courting bouquets that country boys presented to their lady loves. Concoctions of it were also considered good for the hair, to improve its texture and to forestall balding.

A bunch of southernwood sprigs, taken to church, produced a stimulating odor that was supposed to keep listeners awake during overlong sermons.

Branches of the camphor- and lemon-scented species have been hung in closets for hundreds of years as a moth repellent and this practice is still followed today. For this reason, the French call the plant *garde robe* and *armoise.*

Culture

Treated as individual trees, artemisias are charming plants for the window garden. They grow to two feet. I discovered their value in this role quite accidentally when I brought some of them into a cold greenhouse for forcing. I placed one of each species in my plant window and found that they added great interest to the foliage plants already assembled there.

I planted them first in six-inch clay pots, but soon changed to eight-inch pots to balance the expanding tops. Southernwood, as the name indicates, is a very woody plant and this makes it suitable for bonsai treatment. I have two- and three-year-old plants that have already developed miniature gnarled trunks.

Southernwood is not particular about soil. The plants will grow in almost any medium as long as they have light and water. Neither heat nor cold affects them adversely. If brought in from outdoors, they do have a dormant period when the small, soft, needlelike leaves fall, but new leaves soon replace them.

Dittany, dittany of Crete, hop marjoram, *Origanum dictamnus*

The tender plant called dittany is a native of the mountains of Crete and a comparatively new arrival in this country. Its early use was as a wound herb. Legend says that when a mountain goat was shot with arrows, it rushed to a dittany plant and, upon eating it, the arrows were expelled.

Dittany was well known in classical times and Virgil wrote about it. It was the herb which Venus used to cure the wounds of Aeneas. Dittany has also been used as a tea for nervous ailments and as a protection against contagious diseases.

Outdoors, in our climate, dittany is not always a success because wet seasons ruin it, and it is often lost in a large garden.

In my experience, it grows best in the drier atmosphere of the house. Sun is essential to its best growth, and it needs to be separated from other plants so that air can reach its thick gray leaves.

Indoors it reaches a height of six to eight inches.

Dittany is a charming little plant. I like to look at it and remember its ancient uses.

Germander, *Teucrium lucidum* and *chamaedrys*

Early botanists wrote of *Teucrium*, and Dioscorides mentions its use as a medicine by an ancient king of Troy. Germander's use as a cure for gout goes back to the time of the Holy Roman Emperor Charles V, who was reported to have been cured after using a decoction of the herb for sixty days. Its medical use was so highly regarded that it was one of the herbs selected to be grown in the American colonies.

We grow two germanders here. The species *lucidum* is an upright plant with shining leaves that resembles boxwood. *Chamaedrys* is a creeping plant with broader leaves.

Chamaedrys has red-purple or rose flowers on a loose spike and blooms profusely. It is practically indestructible outdoors. *Lucidum*, however, is more attractive as a house plant. It grows upright and stiff and has finely cut dark-green glossy leaves and magenta flowers. It thrives in the sun and likes sharp drainage and sand to grow in, but seems to survive anywhere. I have grown it successfully in almost complete shade.

It reaches twelve inches indoors.

This plant is not to use but to enjoy growing. I prefer it without blossoms outdoors and usually cut them off; indoors, the orchidlike flowers are welcome. *Teucrium* can be trimmed and shaped into a very neat small tree.

Good King Henry, *Chenopodium bonus-henricus*, early spinach, fat hen, bliter, mercury

Chenopodium was once grown in great quantities in England, where it was considered one of the most nutritious of vegetables. Some sources say that it was eaten with chicken and was named for Henry IV of France, who promised a chicken for every pot. It was also used to fatten fowls.

Its name may also refer to magical qualities; it could have been named for Heinz and Heinrich, elves of malicious powers. It is a strange and interesting plant to grow today, although it is now considered of little value as a pot herb.

Indoors it grows to twelve inches.

Heartsease, *Viola tricolor*, Johnny-jump-up, love-in-idleness, wild pansy

Few plants have as many common names as heartsease, the small perennial flower that is the delight of the spring and early-summer garden. The variety of its names indicates its great popularity and wide distribution. In former days it was considered a valuable medicinal herb and was highly esteemed as a heart medicine. It was also used in a potion administered to the lovelorn. A strong syrup of the herb and flowers was reputed to cure skin diseases, and homeopaths have so used it for many years. The plant is, of course, a violet.

For the window garden, bring in a box of tiny self-sown seedlings, planted in the soil in which they grew. Keep them in the sun and they will reward you with tiny blooms in three colors that inspired the name trinity.

Heartsease will grow to eight inches indoors.

Do not hesitate to cut these blossoms. Use them with angelica for cake decorations and on cookies, in wine punch, and with nasturtiums in your salads.

Houseleek, *Sempervivum tectorum*, hen-and-chickens, sedum, stonecrop

The name houseleek comes from the Saxon word *leac,* a plant growing on a house. The plant was once grown on the thatched roofs of houses. Other names denoted various dedications to Thor, Jupiter, and even the devil. It was called Jupiter's-eyes, Jupiter's-beard, and St.-George's-beard. The leaves grow in rosettes three to four inches across and are wedge-shaped, tipped with a soft prickle. Numerous offshoots appear around the parent plant.

In Greece the houseleek was reputed to be a love medicine. Grown on the roofs of houses it was considered a protection against the lightning. It was also believed to afford protection against sorcerers.

As a medicine it was administered in small doses for dysentery, convulsions, and shingles. Externally, it was applied to burns, corns, and warts.

Sedums need a sandy or poor soil, dryness, and full sun. They are interesting to grow and are decorative additions to flower arrangements.

Lovage, *Levisticum officinale*

A native of the mountains of France, Greece, and the Balkan states, lovage came to England early, perhaps with the Romans. In some areas of the British Isles it has become naturalized.

A hardy perennial, it grows to great heights outdoors, three to five feet, and produces great root stocks. The whole plant, leaves and stalk, resembles celery and its flavor is similar.

Lovage was once used medicinally, the roots and seed being particularly valued by the apothecary. It was used by home wine makers to produce a lovage wine and a cordial called lovage which was a mixture of herbs including tansy and yarrow.

Lovage will grow in shade but does need light. Indoors, the plants are dwarfed and present no space problem; they grow about twelve to fourteen inches high.

The tops of the stalks can be added to soups and salads to give them a celery flavor. A tea is sometimes made of their leaves.

Rue, *Ruta graveolens*

Shakespeare wrote, "Rosemary and rue; these keep seeming and savor all the winter long." In the England of that day this was true, because neither of these beloved plants loses its leaves or changes very much until the first hard frosts come and, even then, if there is a little shelter, rue will keep its leaves until spring.

Rue makes a beautiful house plant. The variety 'Blue Beauty' is particularly desirable. It is a compact plant, less branching than the old rue, with incredibly blue-green leaves.

Rue—like lavender, myrtle, and rosemary—is truly a legendary plant, the plant of virtue. It was reputed "to keep maids from going wrong with love." All they had to do was look at it.

In Lithuania and Poland it was the symbol of virginity. Brides wore it pinned to their wedding gowns. Like myrtle, it was reputed to wither when worn by the unchaste. It was also used to exorcise witches.

Culture

To grow rue successfully indoors, start with a small well-rooted plant. (Large old plants from the garden are unsuited to pot culture.) 'Blue Beauty' grows quite rapidly in lean, well-drained soil. It will reach a height of ten to twelve inches.

It can be trained into a topiary tree if you are not allergic to its juice, which can cause dermatitis. I have this allergy for it but it still is one of my favorite plants.

Its Uses

In the past, rue was used in preparing wines and vinegars. In England, it was used in sandwiches. Hung in a doorway it averted the evil eye. It was included in the bouquets given to English judges when they opened a trial and this earned the plant the popular names "judge's plant" and "judge's herb." I use it at Christmas with juniper and rosemary to tie into the ribbons that hold pomander balls. It dries well and will keep for a long time.

Sage, *Salvia leucantha*, Mexican bush sage; *S. coccinea*, Texas sage; *S. sclarea*, clary

Some of the tender sages are candidates for the indoor garden because of their interesting foliage and unusual blossoms. Mexican sage is a giant in the garden but of reasonable size when grown in a pot. The leaves are about six inches long and lance-shaped, white underneath. The flowers are bright lavender and white, in whorled racemes, and look as if they were made of velvet. They dry well for winter bouquets.

Indoors it grows to eighteen inches.

Texas sage is a tender plant with somewhat oval, grayish, hairy leaves two to three inches long, and scarlet blooms in five- to eight-inch racemes.

It grows to ten inches.

Clary has long, broadly oval leaves and pinkish-blue flowers on a spike. I have never grown this species indoors but have heard of its success. It is a biennial.

Santolina, *Santolina viridis*, and *chamaecyparissus*

Green santolina (*viridis*) is a stunning hardy shrub from the Mediterranean, an ornament to the garden indoors or out. Little has been written about it but, once grown, it will enchant you. It grows a foot or two tall and has bright yellow-green finely cut leaves and compact yellow-button flowers.

Outdoors, it enlarges each year so that there are many side shoots to pull if you wish to start young plants indoors. Plants can be grown from cuttings also. For indoor growing use small plants. Pot them in three-inch pots and they will not need to be moved for a year. The plants will need some sun and good air circulation.

Indoors it grows from twelve to eighteen inches high.

Santolina produces an oil with a strong resinous odor which has been used commercially in polishes. Grow it for its attractive foliage and interesting flowers.

Gray santolina (*chamaecyparissus*) is often called lavender cotton, though it is in no way related to the cotton plant or to lavender. In the early days and through the eighteenth century it was used like southernwood to keep moths away from clothing. Medicinally, it was used as a vermifuge and in an eye lotion. In Culpeper's time, it was reputed to "resist poison, putrefaction and heal the biting of venomous beasts."

It is impossible for me to imagine an herb garden indoors or out without gray santolina. Its finely cut leaves, crowded closely on stiff stems, resemble coral.

Gray santolina needs a lean soil and a maximum amount of sun to be at its best. If it is trained properly, it will grow upright like a little tree, to a height of ten to twelve inches. If allowed to grow in its own fashion, it will spill pleasantly over the edge of a container. And it is good in mixed plantings.

For best window-garden results, don't overwater this plant. Carefully cut off dead leaves and bits of brown that may collect at times. Give it air; avoid crowding it with other plants.

Like green santolina, this plant is mainly decorative. Its gray-coral branches are attractive in flower arrangements. We use it in living wreaths of green herbs and in Advent wreaths. If such wreaths are kept moist, they will often serve as a rooting medium for gray santolina.

Tansy, *Tanacetum vulgare, T. crispum*

Tansy is an Old World herb which was brought to New England by the colonists. It was planted by the kitchen door, partly to be at hand for use and partly to keep away ants and flies.

The botanical name is from the Greek, meaning "immortality." It may have been selected because the plant was used at funerals, because its flowers are long-lasting, or because a drink made with tansy was believed to ensure immortality.

Tansy-flavored cakes, called tansies, were served at Easter and were thought to purify the blood after the rigors of a Lenten diet. They were also eaten in remembrance of the bitter herbs of the Jewish Passover. Use of the herb as a tea was largely American. Tansy tea was a favorite colonial remedy, reputed to cure such diversified ailments as worms in children, hysteria, gout, fevers, and the measles.

Tansy has enjoyed a great surge of popularity recently because of the interest in organic gardening. It finds a place in "companion plantings" and is said to bring health to the garden by repelling insects. Like camomile, it acts as the plants' physician.

Grow tansy inside only if an outdoor garden is impossible, as it is a hardy plant. For indoor growing, the fernleaf species (*crispum*) does particularly well. Its growth is less rampant than that of *vulgare* and its leaves are like green lace. *Crispum* does not flower as profusely as *vulgare* but it is too much to expect blooms of any consequence in a house planting. Two pots of tansy are ample, one of each kind.

It grows to eighteen inches high indoors.

Tansy grows new leaves rapidly, so they can be cut frequently. Dry them and use them to prevent moth damage.

Flowering Herbs

Many herbs have inconspicuous flowers or do not blossom indoors. I recommend the following two plants for interesting flowers about all winter:

Elfin herb, *Cuphea hyssopifolia,* a native of Mexico and Guatemala, is a charmer with dark-green shiny leaves resembling those of hyssop and purplish-pink or white flowers. Its ultimate growth is one foot and it is a hardy house plant.

African baby's-breath, *Chaenostoma fastigiatum,* a native of South Africa, has very finely cut dark-green strongly scented foliage. It is covered with white flowers winter and summer, and grows well under almost all conditions. Indoors it ultimately grows twelve inches high.

Gray-leafed Accents

Herbs with gray foliage provide an interesting contrast among green-leafed plants in the window garden and some have already been mentioned. I especially like the following three:

Senecio cineraria, dusty-miller, a branching perennial with leaves cut in narrow rounded lobes. It grows ten to twelve inches high indoors.

The licorice plant, *Helichrysum petiolatum,* with trailing stems, wooly white leaves rounded at the tips, and white flowers. This herb has a faint licorice smell. It is good for hanging baskets.

The curry plant, *Helichrysum angustifolium,* with leaves that are almost white. Its growth resembles lavender, and it has a strong odor of curry. It will reach a height of twelve inches indoors and is broad and spreading.

6

Herbs Make the Party

Herbs, with their legendary associations and hidden meanings, can often make your party an outstanding success. They are especially appropriate as decorations, favors, and gifts at Valentine parties and showers for brides.

The language of plants was well understood in the Victorian era and was used in charming ways. Often the parlor table was graced by a small book decorated with an embossed design of flowers which listed the meanings of different plants. By ar-

How to make a tussie-mussie: Above, a twelve-inch paper doily is pierced in the center so a heavy paper cone or florist's cup filled with flowers (below) can be inserted, the whole then decorated with ribbon.

ranging flowers and foliage carefully, a small bouquet could be made which conveyed a message. The message could be sentimental, revealing various degrees of love and esteem; it could administer a sly dig, convey sympathy, or reprove the bold or overpompous.

Such bouquets were called tussie-mussies. Originally, the tussie-mussie was contained in a richly ornamented holder of gold or silver filigree or china. Sometimes it was surrounded by lace ruffles tied with ribbons. Always, the flower in the center was the keynote. Around it were arranged meaningful flowers and foliage of lesser import.

Valentine Party

For a Valentine party, especially a party for a bride near this date, design a tussie-mussie for each guest. In this case the theme will be sentimental love and good wishes.

For the center use a rose. If a fresh bloom is not available, use one of the fragrant dried French roses. The rose is a symbol of love, a rosebud specifically of young love. Wire the rose, leaving ends that can be twined around the other components of the bouquet.

Plants encircling the rose could be: rosemary for remembrance, your presence revives me; myrtle, love and domestic happiness; ivy, constancy and friendship; rose geranium, preference; marjoram, blushes and happiness; sage, domestic virtue and immortality; heartsease or wild violet, the Valentine herb, thought.

This group makes an attractive bouquet. I sometimes add a small cellophane package of frankincense, which I tie in the center under the rose. The meaning of frankincense is incense of a faithful heart, also gladness. Other geraniums that could be used are: apple, present preference; ivy, I engage you for the next dance; nutmeg, an unexpected meeting.

Sentiments that can be expressed by still other flowers and foliage are:

Camomile, humility, triumph in adversity
Daffodil, regard
Heliotrope, devotion and faithfulness
Holly, am I forgotten?
Iris, my compliments
Jasmine, I attach myself to you
Juniper, protection
Lily-of-the-valley, a return to happiness
Mignonette, your qualities surpass your charms
Mint, wisdom
Mugwort, happiness and protection
Peppermint, warmth and cordiality
Pink, fascination
Rue, clear vision and understanding
Southernwood, dreams of a lover

How to Construct

Use a large red heart for a background. On it glue a paper-lace doily to serve as a holder. Puncture two holes in the center of the paper heart, insert a white ribbon, and pull the two ends together on the front of the heart, allowing enough ribbon to tie the bouquet with a generous bow.

Wrap the ends of the green plant materials in foil. Place the rose in the center, tie in with the ribbon the wrapped stems of other plants, and make a bow to cover them. Write the meaning of the herbs you have used on the back of the Valentine. This makes a delightful memento for a guest, a fragrant lasting sachet.

If red does not fit your color scheme, use a white or gold heart. Net could be used instead of ribbon.

A Party in May

If the party comes in May or at Easter time, use tiny May baskets as favors. These baskets are made of splints and come in natural colors. The same arrangement of foliage and flowers can be used. Attach a small card giving the symbolic meanings of the plants you use.

The Table Centerpiece

A wreath of scented-geranium leaves makes an attractive centerpiece for your party. You will need a wire planting form, sphagnum moss, and leaves. Fill the form with moist moss, then wet it thoroughly. Place it on a round tray and insert in the moss tip ends and leaves until the form is filled in. If the moss is kept moist afterward, the geraniums will often root and you can pot them.

Place small flowers in the wreath if any are available. Set the punch bowl in the center.

An ivy ring is also appropriate. Ivy symbolizes friendship, fidelity, marriage, constancy, and good wine.

A Shower of Herbs

My artist, Kathleen Burke, told me of a recent bridal shower she attended in which herbs played a leading role. For the gourmet cook such a shower would be delightful and very practical. Here are some gift suggestions.

Herb Rack

A rack for the kitchen, containing the basic seasonings, would be useful. Include anise, coriander, cumin, caraway, cardamom, basil, dill seed and dill weed, rosemary, savory, thyme, tarragon, marjoram, orégano, and garlic powder. A small rack could be included, containing mixed seasonings for salads, poultry, spaghetti and other Italian dishes; for fish, and fine herbs for omelets and other egg recipes.

Vinegars

A set of herb vinegars would include tarragon, basil, garlic, and dill. To this list can be added exotic kinds that are not essential but fun to try. I suggest a strong mint vinegar, very good for a mint sauce or a fruit salad; rose-geranium vinegar, made by adding leaves and rose coloring to vinegar (leave the leaves in and it will be as pretty as a picture), excellent for Near East dishes that call for rose water, which is often unavailable; shallot vinegar, which is delicious but not usually included in commercial collections; and burnet vinegar, with its cucumber flavor.

Aromatic Toilet Vinegar

Combine 2 cups dried rose petals, 1 cup dried lavender flowers, ¼ cup dried jasmine blossoms, and ¼ cup dried rosemary leaves. Mix well, place in a glass jar, and pour in 1 quart of white vinegar. Put on a tight cover. Shake well. Let set for a day, then add 1 cup rose water. Let stand for 2 weeks. Strain and bottle. Makes about 1½ quarts.

Shallots and Chives

Shallots packaged in an open-mesh onion bag make another interesting gift. Tie on some good recipes for sauces and other concoctions. Shallots keep well in a cool, dry, airy place. Along with them, give a jar of the freeze-dried type which, if kept dry and tightly covered, will retain their flavor indefinitely. A jar of freeze-dried chives could also be included. Freeze-dried products don't need refrigeration—in fact they may be ruined by it. Just keep them on a shelf in a warm, dry kitchen. Warn the recipient of these gifts to keep all green herbs in tightly closed containers and not to place them in the sun or in strong light. Such treatment fades their lovely green color, although the flavor remains. Chives, parsley, basil, and marjoram fade very quickly.

Spice Rack

A spice rack would round out the kitchen collection. I like large jars for spices that are in constant use. I also like them whole rather than ground, and I find that many brides are going back to their grandmothers' day for recipes that call for such special products as whole nutmeg, whole ginger, stick cinnamon, vanilla beans, cardamom in shells, whole cloves, allspice, peppercorns, and mace. Apothecary jars filled with these unusual items are both decorative and useful. Nutmegs could be combined with a grater, peppercorns (both white and black) with a pepper mill. Vanilla beans could be placed in sugar as a suggestion for their use. Small cinnamon sticks will fit into such a jar, but the long sticks used as stirrers in hot punch will not. I tie them with a bow of colorful calico.

Candied Angelica

Candied angelica is not easy to find, but it is always good to have on hand for cake and Christmas bread, or as a decoration for cookies. This is best kept in cellophane. For giving, tie it with a bow and include a recipe for stollen or a birthday cake. Correctly candied, angelica will keep forever.

Cookbooks

One of the best of gifts is a shelf of cookbooks, which might include a hand-made one with a favorite recipe supplied by each guest. If you have time to make such a book, this is how it is done.

Buy a looseleaf notebook and cover it with an herb wallpaper, an herb towel or place mats, seed packages, or a calico herbal print. For illustration inside to emphasize each herb, illustrations from seed envelopes are useful. Thus you could start with anise, using a picture of it and telling its story, if you have that much time. Each recipe could be signed by the giver.

Herb Chart

Another idea is an herb chart that can be posted inside a cupboard or hung on the kitchen wall as a decorative note.

Window Plants

If the bride's kitchen has room for a window planter or pots of herbs, do provide a few useful plants. However, it is best to arrange for someone to keep them until the bride returns from her honeymoon and is settled in her new home. Otherwise, growing things might present her with a problem.

Fragrant Herbs

Fragrant herbs for bureau drawers—of rose potpourri, lavender, and spicy mixtures to keep moths away—would be other welcome gifts at a shower. Flat sachets to place in stacks of sheets are a good idea. Make them of organdy, silk, or lace if you wish them to be elegant. For those who like Early American things, make them of calico or use a plain material and appliqué a quaint scene from a piece of toile. There are toiles printed with garden scenes, shepherdesses, and lovelorn swains.

Pomander Balls

Pomander balls—oranges or apples closely studded with cloves, rolled in spice, and tied in net with ribbons and sprays of rosemary or other fragrant herbs—are a perfect gift for the clothes closet. A wreath of dried scented herbs and flowers could be used in a bedroom or bathroom.

A Fragrant House

Make your home fragrant for the bridal shower. Burn an incense mixture of frankincense and myrrh with spices such as cinnamon, cloves, vetiver, and lavender on the simmering burner of your stove or on the hearth. (In a small apartment, burn only a pinch.) The younger generation is taking an interest in odors. Many who are versed in fragrance will prefer these natural odors of barks, berries, and gums to the commercial sprays that are available.

Part Two

Recipes with Herbs

VALENTINE PUNCH BOWL

This tangy, refreshing, and *stimulating* mixture tastes rather like a daiquiri, but a punch avoids the difficulty of serving cocktails for a crowd. The bright color adds a festive note to any holiday table at Christmas and New Year's, as well as at this February festival.

Combine 1 fifth of white rum, 1 fifth of vodka, 1 quart cranberry juice, the juice of 4 limes (or 4 lemons), and ½ cup sugar, or more to taste. Mix well and chill in the refrigerator until serving time. Then, as needed, pour over a big cake of ice in a punch bowl. Set this on a tray decorated with a wreath of herbs made from the plants in your window garden.

SHRIMP BUTTER SPREAD

Favorite party food.

1 pound frozen shrimp
½ pound (2 sticks) butter
½ teaspoon salt
½ teaspoon finely ground pepper
¼ teaspoon grated mace
1 teaspoon chili powder

Cook shrimp and chop fine. Work into a paste with the other ingredients and serve as a spread on crackers. *Makes about 12 servings.*

ALMOND BACON CANAPÉ

Good with drinks for the bridal shower.

6 slices bacon
¼ cup slivered almonds
¼ cup sesame seeds
1 3-ounce package cream cheese
2 tablespoons chopped chives
1 teaspoon chopped Egyptian onion tops
¼ cup butter

Sauté bacon until crisp and drain on paper toweling. Toast almonds and sesame seeds in a heavy skillet until brown, taking care not to burn. Allow to cool. Mix all ingredients together and put in refrigerator to mellow. Spread on sesame or small whole-wheat crackers. *Makes 12 canapés.*

CHRISTMAS CANAPÉ

Serve this with crackers or as a relish. The tangy taste is excellent with holiday foods but good at any time of year.

A lavabo with plants of mint, rosemary, thyme, and sweet marjoram

Party punch bowl with a wreath of ivy accented with roses; the tussie mussie at the lower left

At the left, a standard rose geranium; above right, a myrtle in topiary form; below right, rosemary trained as a bonsai

The author's winter window garden of herbs in an alcove with a presiding Saint Francis

1 1-pound box cranberries
1 cup sugar
1 pint creamed cottage cheese
1 5-ounce jar horseradish

Cook cranberries in water to cover until they pop. Add sugar and cook until sugar is dissolved and mixture thickens. Remove from heat, cool, and add the cottage cheese and horseradish. *Serves 12 generously.*

CRANBERRY SPREAD

This is a nice pink spread for a Valentine party but attractive at any time of year.

1 1-pound box cranberries
1 cup sugar
1 cup (8 ounces) cream cheese
1 5-ounce jar horseradish
2 cups cottage cheese

Cook cranberries with sugar until mixture thickens. Let it cool. Stir in the cream cheese and horseradish. Let set in refrigerator for 1 hour. Drain off excess juice and add 2 cups cottage cheese, or enough to thicken mixture to spreading consistency.

CREAM-CHEESE MINT BALLS

¼ cup sesame seeds
½ cup finely ground almonds
1 cup (8-ounce package) cream cheese
¼ cup chopped fresh mint leaves
½ teaspoon salt
3 tablespoons brandy

In a skillet, toast sesame seeds and almonds, taking care not to burn them, then pulverize in a mixing bowl, blend the cheese, mint, salt, and brandy. Form the cheese mixture into balls, about 1 teaspoon each. Roll in the almond-and-sesame mixture until well coated. Place each cheese ball on a mint leaf and serve with sesame crackers. *Makes about 18.*

EXOTICA SPREAD

- 1 3-ounce package almonds
- ½ cup sesame seeds
- 1 cup (8-ounce package) cream cheese
- 1 banana, mashed
- 1 3½-ounce can shredded coconut
- ½ cup smooth peanut butter
- ½ cup sweet relish
- ¼ cup minced fresh parsley
- ¼ teaspoon cumin seeds

Toast the almonds and sesame seeds in a skillet. Mix together the cheese, banana, coconut, and peanut butter, and work in the almonds and sesame seeds. Add the sweet relish, parsley, and cumin seeds, and blend until smooth. Store in small jars in the refrigerator to have ready to serve on crackers. *Makes about 2 cups.*

SALMON SOUP WITH HERBS

In turquoise-blue or green bowls this looks delightful sprinkled with paprika and garnished with chopped parsley. A lemon slice, garnished with parsley, may be fastened to the side of each bowl or a very thin slice of lemon sprinkled with parsley or dill placed in the center of each one.

- 1 1-pound can red salmon
- ¼ pound (1 stick) butter
- 1 clove garlic, crushed
- 1 cup chopped celery
- 2 tablespoons chopped onion tops
- 2 tablespoons flour
- 1 cup cream
- 1 cup milk
- Salt
- Pepper
- ¼ cup chopped or flaked parsley
- ⅛ teaspoon finely cut tarragon or dill weed
- Paprika

Drain and flake salmon, removing dark skin and bones. Reserve liquid. Cook salmon in butter in a heavy skillet. Add garlic, celery, and onion tops. Simmer until soft. Blend flour with cream and milk and stir in with parsley and tarragon or dill weed. Add the salmon liquid and salt and pepper to taste. For a thinner soup add extra milk and cream or evaporated milk to make up to 1 quart. *Serves 6.*

GREEN HERB SOUP

- 1 cup chopped sorrel leaves
- 1 cup chopped spinach
- ¼ cup chopped parsley
- 2 stalks lovage and tops, chopped
- 2 stalks celery and tops, chopped
- 2 onions, chopped
- 1 clove garlic
- ¼ pound (1 stick) butter
- 1 13¾-ounce can chicken broth
- 3 large potatoes, peeled and sliced
- 1 teaspoon salt
- Pepper

Combine sorrel, spinach, parsley, lovage, celery, onions, and garlic. Add to butter in a deep soup kettle. Cook until greens are limp and butter starts to brown. Discard garlic. Add chicken broth and potatoes. Cover and simmer 30 minutes. For a smooth soup, run through a blender. Pour into bouillon cups. *Serves 8 to 10.*

For cream soup, add 2 10½-ounce cans cream of chicken soup blended with 2 tablespoons flour.

SORREL AND SPINACH SOUP

Sorrel grows well indoors, and a large plant will supply leaves for several pots of soup.

- 2 onions, chopped
- 1 cup chopped sorrel leaves
- 2 cups chopped spinach, well packed
- ¼ cup butter
- 2 potatoes, peeled and cubed
- 1 sprig rosemary
- Salt
- Pepper
- Dash of garlic powder
- 2 cups water
- 3 cups chicken broth
- 2 egg yolks
- 1 cup heavy cream
- Butter
- Grated nutmeg
- Chives, chopped
- Rosemary, chopped

Sauté onions, sorrel, and spinach in butter until onions are golden and leaves are limp. Add potatoes, rosemary, seasonings, and water. Simmer until leaves are soft enough to sieve for a purée. Place purée in a kettle with the chicken broth, and simmer for 10 minutes. Remove from heat and let cool a little. Beat egg yolks into the cream and add very slowly (to prevent curdling) to *lukewarm* broth mixture. Stir with a whisk until blended. Reheat *but do not boil.* Dot with butter, sprinkle grated nutmeg on top, and serve with a garnish of chives and rosemary. *Serves 6 to 8.*

TUNA-MUSHROOM CHOWDER WITH HERBS

- 1 13-ounce can white tuna
- ¼ pound (1 stick) butter
- ½ cup chopped celery
- 1 onion, chopped
- 2 tablespoons chopped green onion tops
- 1 cup canned sliced mushrooms
- 3 medium potatoes, peeled and cubed
- 1 tablespoon chopped parsley
- ½ teaspoon marjoram
- 1 large sprig thyme, chopped
- ⅛ teaspoon freshly ground pepper
- Salt
- 2 cups water
- 4 cups milk, or 2 cups cream and 2 cups milk

Heat tuna, butter, celery, onion, onion tops, mushrooms, potatoes, and seasonings with water to cover. Cook slowly until potatoes are done. Separately, heat milk or milk and cream until warm. Stir into the tuna mixture. Serve with large chowder crackers toasted with garlic butter. *Serves 6.*

GREEK RICE

- ¼ cup butter
- 2 onions, chopped
- 1 clove garlic, crushed
- 4 tablespoons chopped parsley
- ½ cup canned sliced mushrooms
- 1 cup canned tomatoes
- 4 small link sausages, skinned and chopped

1½ cups cooked rice
3 cups chicken stock
1 teaspoon oregano
2 teaspoons basil
1 teaspoon salt
½ teaspoon freshly ground pepper
¼ cup melted butter
¾ cup cooked peas
4 tablespoons raisins, sauteed in butter

Melt the butter in an ovenproof casserole. Add the onions and cook until soft but not brown. Add the garlic, parsley, mushrooms, tomatoes, and sausages. Simmer for about 20 minutes, or until sausages are well cooked. Stir in the rice, chicken stock, herbs, and seasonings. Cover tightly and cook for about 30 minutes in a 350° F. oven. Turn into a shallow bowl, toss with a fork, and mix in the melted butter, peas, and raisins. *Serves 6.*

MEAT LOAF DE LUXE WITH LOVAGE

1½ pounds top round steak, ground
4 small link sausages, skinned and cut up
1 large onion, grated
1 egg, beaten
½ cup cream
1 cup fine bread crumbs
1 tablespoon chopped celery
1 tablespoon chopped lovage, leaves and stalk
1 teaspoon salt
½ teaspoon pepper
2 teaspoons red wine

Reserving ¼ cup of the ground beef, make a smooth mixture of the rest of the beef with the sausage, onion, and egg. Add cream to bread crumbs with celery, lovage, salt, pepper, and red wine. Shape into loaf. Bake in a 350° F. oven for 1½ hours.

Sauce
¼ cup beef
1 clove garlic
2 tablespoons flour
2 slices bacon, cut
1 cup beer
1 cup tomato paste
1 tablespoon dill seed
½ teaspoon basil
1 bay leaf
1 cup sliced stuffed olives

Garnish
Whole stuffed olives
Parsley sprigs
Chopped chives

Sauté the beef with the garlic in a little oil; discard the garlic.

Stir in the flour. Brown the mixture with the bacon. Add the beer and tomato paste. Cook, stirring constantly, until the sauce thickens. Season with the dill, basil, and bay leaf. Cover and cook for about 15 minutes. Stir in the sliced olives.

Turn the meat loaf out on a serving platter and pour the sauce over it. Garnish with whole stuffed olives, parsley sprigs, and chopped chives. Serve with noodles, spaghetti, or rice. *Serves 6.*

MINTED LAMB

- 1 6-pound leg of lamb
- 1 teaspoon salt
- 1 teaspoon freshly ground pepper
- 1 clove garlic, crushed, or ¼ teaspoon garlic powder
- ½ cup flour
- 1 cup chicken stock
- 1 cup dry white wine
- 2 small onions, chopped
- ¼ cup finely chopped spearmint leaves
- Fresh mint leaves
- 1 tablespoon chopped green onion tops

Rub the lamb with a mixture of salt, pepper, garlic, and flour. Line an open roasting pan with a piece of foil large enough to fold over the lamb. Place in pan; pour over it the chicken stock and wine; sprinkle on the onions and spearmint leaves. Fold the foil over the lamb, and roast in a preheated 375° F. oven for about 1 hour. Every 15 minutes for the next hour, open the foil and baste the lamb. If you wish it to brown, leave the foil open; if not, close the foil until the last 15 minutes. Heat a platter. Remove the lamb to the platter and garnish with the mint leaves and onion tops. Good served with mint jelly and parsley-butter potatoes. *Serves 6 to 8.*

PARSLEY-ONION SQUARES

Good with supper or for cocktails.

- 2 cups sliced onions
- ¼ cup butter
- 2 cups sifted flour
- 2 teaspoons baking powder
- 1 teaspoon salt
- ¼ cup shortening

1 cup milk
¼ cup parsley flakes
½ teaspoon marjoram
⅓ cup sour cream
2 tablespoons chives

In a skillet, cook onions in butter until they are transparent. Let cool. Sift together flour, baking powder, and salt; cut in shortening. Gradually add milk with parsley and marjoram. (Or substitute poultry seasoning.) Stir only enough to blend. Turn the dough into a well-buttered 8-inch square pan. Spread the onion mixture over the dough, then the sour cream, and sprinkle with chives. Bake in a preheated 425° F. oven for 20 minutes or until fairly firm. Cut into squares and serve hot or cold with or without butter. *Serves 12.*

PILAF WITH CHICKEN AND HERBS

6 chicken breasts
6 cups water
¼ teaspoon rosemary
½ cup olive oil
½ cup minced onions
1 clove garlic
1 teaspoon black pepper
6 cardamom seeds, crushed
2 cups uncooked rice
2 cups cooked chopped ham
1 cup stuffed olives, chopped or halved
½ cup chopped green onions
1 tablespoon paprika
1 tablespoon butter
½ cup chopped parsley
4 packages frozen peas, cooked

Cook chicken breasts in water with rosemary until tender. (Meat should separate easily from bones.) Reserve 4 cups chicken stock. In a deep skillet (which has a cover for later use), heat olive oil. Add onions, garlic, pepper, cardamom, then rice. Cook uncovered until onions are soft and golden. Discard garlic. Gradually add chicken stock, cover tightly, and cook over low heat until rice is done and has absorbed all the stock. (Check occasionally to be sure rice is not sticking.) Cube the chicken. Combine chicken, chopped ham, olives, green onions, paprika, butter, and parsley. Toss slightly with fork. Turn onto a large heated platter and garnish with a ring of peas. *Serves 12.*

A cold vegetable plate for accompaniment: Arrange 12 stalks celery hearts, 12 artichoke hearts, 2 large sliced Italian onions, and 1 cup large stuffed olives on a platter. Sprinkle on a little finely chopped parsley and 1 teaspoon chopped chives.

PORK CASSEROLE WITH HERBS

6 center-cut pork chops
½ cup flour
½ teaspoon salt
2 teaspoons caraway seeds
1 teaspoon parsley
Pinch of garlic powder
¼ cup butter
2 to 3 cups dry white wine
¼ cup butter
6 slices bread, crumbled
2 green onions, chopped fine
½ teaspoon poultry seasoning
¼ cup water
6 potatoes, peeled and sliced
⅛ pound (½ stick) butter
Salt
Pepper
Paprika

Roll the chops in a mixture of flour, salt, caraway seeds, parsley, and garlic powder. Melt the ¼ cup butter in a skillet, put in chops, sprinkle any leftover seasoning mixture over them, and sauté on both sides until brown. Pour in 1 cup of the wine and cover to cook until done, about 1 hour. (Add more wine if necessary to prevent scorching.)

In another pan, make a dressing of ¼ cup butter, the crumbled bread, onions, poultry seasoning, and ¼ cup water. Cook until moisture is absorbed and crumbs begin to brown.

Move chops to a casserole and spread the dressing over them, adding enough wine to cover the bottom of the dish. Arrange potato slices over the dressing, melt the half stick of butter, pour it over the potatoes, season with salt and pepper and sprinkle with paprika. Bake in a preheated 350° F. oven until potatoes are done—about 30 minutes. Serve at the table from the casserole. *Serves 6.*

ONION PIE

Pie shell
1½ cups flour
1½ cups butter
½ teaspoon salt
¼ cup chopped green sage
2 teaspoons chopped chives

Filling

5 cups finely chopped onions
6 slices bacon, cut up
1 cup butter
¾ cup heavy cream
3 tablespoons flour
4 eggs, lightly beaten
Salt
Pepper

Blend flour, butter, salt, sage, and chives with your hands until mixture can be easily kneaded. (Cold water may have to be added but very little.) Set dough aside for 30 minutes. Then roll on a floured board to ⅛-inch thickness. Line an 8-inch square pan with the dough.

Sauté onions and bacon in butter for 15 minutes or until onions are golden brown. Cool slightly. Slowly add cream blended with flour, eggs, salt, and pepper. Stir with a whisk until smooth. Turn into the pastry shell and bake in a preheated 350° F. oven for about 25 minutes or until custard is set. *Serves 6.*

OYSTERS WITH CHERVIL

This is an excellent main dish for a Valentine's Day Party.

2 pints oysters
6 to 8 slices bread, crumbled fine
3 egg yolks, well beaten
1 pint light cream
⅛ teaspoon mace
2 tablespoons chervil or finely chopped parsley
Salt
Pepper
1 tablespoon lemon juice
1 teaspoon grated lemon
2 tablespoons flour
2 tablespoons butter

Divide oysters into separate pints and drain, reserving ¼ cup liquid. Chop 1 pint very fine and add the oyster liquid. Dry the second pint of oysters on paper toweling. Spread out crumbled bread on waxed paper, reserving about 1 tablespoon for garnish. Dip oysters in egg, then in crumbs, and turn into buttered 2-quart casserole. In double boiler, heat cream until lukewarm and add chopped oysters with seasonings, lemon juice, and rind. Add flour and 1 tablespoon of the butter. Stir with whisk until mixture thickens. Pour over the oysters in the casserole. Sprinkle reserved bread crumbs on top, and dot with the rest of the butter. Bake in a preheated 350° F. oven for 30 minutes. *Serves 12.*

QUICK SUPPER DISH

- 2½ ounces dried beef, shredded
- ¼ pound (1 stick) sweet butter
- 2 tablespoons flour
- 1 cup light cream
- 2 tablespoons chopped Egyptian onions
- Salt
- Pepper
- Chopped chives
- Chopped parsley

Lightly sauté beef in butter. Add flour and stir until absorbed and the mixture creamy. Slowly add light cream, Egyptian onions, salt and pepper to taste. Heat thoroughly. Serve over baked potatoes that have been split as soon as done and the contents mashed, or over rice or toast. Garnish with chopped chives. Sprinkle a little chopped parsley over all. *Serves 4.*

STUFFED ARTICHOKE HEARTS

For this you will need the canned cooked artichoke hearts that come from Italy. They are packed in brine, easy to work with, and delicious.

These are good cold or hot. Serve with slices of tomato or a tomato sauce if you wish, though I like them plain. For groups (you will have to increase the quantity), make a casserole of the browned artichokes, cover with tomato sauce, and sprinkle with sweet basil. Heat for about 20 minutes in a 350° F. oven.

- ½ cup canned sliced mushrooms
- 1 14-ounce can Italian artichokes (10 to 12 hearts)
- 2 eggs, well beaten
- 1 teaspoon flour
- 1 cup fine bread crumbs
- 1 sprig rosemary, finely chopped
- ⅛ teaspoon poultry seasoning
- Pinch of garlic
- 1 cup minced ham (sliced Danish sandwich ham or Italian hot ham)
- ½ pound (2 sticks) butter
- ½ cup minced parsley
- 10 to 12 sprigs rosemary

Drain mushrooms and set aside. Make a batter with the eggs, flour, and bread crumbs. Stir in rosemary, poultry seasoning, and garlic. Sauté mushrooms in half the butter, chop fine, and add to minced ham. Stuff the artichokes with the mushroom-ham mixture, making as small an opening as possible. Roll the artichokes in the batter until coated. Sauté in remaining butter until golden brown. Sprinkle artichokes with parsley and put a sprig of rosemary on top of each one. *Serves 6.*

PINEAPPLE-MINT JELLIED SALAD

Nice for the bridal shower.

- 1 small box lime-flavored gelatin
- 1 small box lemon-flavored gelatin
- 1 envelope unflavored gelatin
- 2 cups hot water
- 1 cup mixed canned fruits
- 1 1-pound 4-ounce can crushed pineapple
- 1 cup chopped mint leaves (several kinds)
- 1 8-ounce package cream cheese
- ½ cup mayonnaise
- 1 cup white wine
- 1 cup lemon and lime juice
- 2 drops mint extract

Dissolve gelatin in hot water. Drain mixed fruits and pineapple, reserving juices. Stew mint leaves in the fruit juices for 10 minutes. Blend cheese into hot gelatin mixture. Stir in mayonnaise, fruits, wine, lemon-lime juice, and mint extract. Pour into a round 2-quart mold and a heart-shaped 1-pint mold (this smaller mold for future use). Refrigerate until firm. Turn out the larger mold onto a platter. Decorate with a garland made from the herbs growing in your window garden—pineapple mint, apple mint, and pineapple sage, this last for its delectable odor. *The large mold serves 12.*

KIDNEY BEAN SALAD

For a complete luncheon, serve sliced ham with this salad, or a platter of cold cuts with a sprinkling of finely cut celery tops and chives and slices of sweet Italian onions. Sometimes I add chopped ham to the salad for easier serving to large groups.

1 1-pound can kidney beans
1 5-ounce jar horseradish
¼ cup sweet relish
1 tablespoon chopped Egyptian onion tops
1 tablespoon finely chopped chives
½ teaspoon chili powder
½ cup powdered pimientos
1 clove garlic, crushed, or ¼ teaspoon garlic powder
1 teaspoon savory
½ cup sour cream
1 cup chopped celery
2 cups finely chopped lettuce

Drain beans and remove pieces of pork. Add horseradish, relish, onion tops, chives (from your window plants), chili powder, pimientos, garlic, and savory. Then stir in sour cream, and lettuce. *Serves 6 to 8.*

CHEESE BREAD WITH DILL AND TANSY

2 cups boiling water
½ cup grated Parmesan cheese
1 7½-ounce jar sweet red peppers, chopped
⅓ cup butter
¾ cup sugar
¼ cup dill weed
1 tablespoon chopped chives
2 tablespoons chopped green tansy
2 yeast cakes
¼ cup lukewarm water
1 teaspoon sugar
4 eggs, well beaten
5 cups sifted flour
Extra butter

In a bowl, pour the boiling water over the cheese, peppers, butter, ¾ cup sugar, dill, chives, and tansy. Let cool. Soften yeast in the lukewarm water with the 1 teaspoon sugar. To cooled cheese mixture, add eggs and softened yeast. Blend in flour to make a soft and workable batter. Turn onto a floured board and knead well. Place in a warmed bowl and let rise until double in bulk. With buttered hands, mold dough into 3 loaves. Place in 5 by 9-inch bread pans, and rub loaves with butter. Let rise again until double in bulk. Bake in a preheated 375° F. oven for 10 minutes. Reduce heat to 300° F. and bake for about 40 minutes longer. *Each loaf makes about 20 slices.*

LEMON CORIANDER LOAF

- ½ cup sugar
- 2 eggs
- 2 cups milk
- Juice and rind of 1 lemon
- 3¼ cups flour
- 4½ teaspoons baking powder
- ½ teaspoon salt
- ¼ cup coriander seeds (whole or crushed)

Cream sugar and eggs together. Stir in milk and juice and rind of lemon. Sift flour, baking powder, and salt together. Add to first mixture. Add coriander seeds, and beat for 5 minutes. Pour into 2 well-buttered 5 by 9-inch bread pans. Bake in a preheated moderate (350° F.) oven for 30 minutes, or until firm in center. *Makes approximately 24 slices.*

Frosting and decoration. Mix together 2 cups confectioners' sugar, 3½ teaspoons lemon juice, ½ teaspoon grated lemon rind, and spread over each loaf. If you wish, decorate with a daisy of slivered almonds, coriander seeds for the center, angelica strips for leaves and stem.

NUT BREAD WITH SESAME SEEDS

This bread cuts better the second day. For party fare, bake a large loaf and spread with whipped cream cheese mixed with raisins or currants, a little sugar, and some vanilla extract. Or make 2 smaller loaves and put them together with the cream cheese mixture. Sometimes we toast extra sesame seeds to add to the cream cheese or just to sprinkle over it.

- 6 eggs, separated
- 1 cup sugar
- 1 teaspoon baking powder
- 1 cup bread crumbs, packed
- Juice of 1 lemon
- 1 cup walnut pieces
- 1 3-ounce package sliced almonds
- ½ cup sesame seeds
- 1 teaspoon brandy

Beat egg yolks until light. Add sugar and beat until foamy. Combine baking powder and bread crumbs and stir into egg-sugar mixture. Stir in lemon juice. Add walnuts, almonds, sesame seeds, and brandy. Beat egg whites until they form stiff peaks. Fold into batter. For 1 large loaf, bake in a 9 by 5-inch loaf pan; for 2 smaller loaves, use the same pans with less dough in each. Butter pans well or line with buttered wax paper. Bake in a preheated slow (about 300° F.) oven for 40 minutes for the large loaf; about 30 for the smaller ones. Let cool before removing from pans. *Makes about 25 slices.*

ORANGE BREAD WITH CORIANDER

This is even better the second day. Nice with orange frosting and a decoration of candied fruits or orange peel, or with angelica.

1 orange
Boiling water
1 cup raisins
2 eggs, well beaten
1 cup sugar
¼ cup coriander seeds (whole)
½ cup chopped nuts
¼ cup shortening
2 cups flour
1 teaspoon baking powder
1 teaspoon baking soda

Squeeze the orange and add enough boiling water to the juice to make 1 cup of liquid. Grind the orange peel with the raisins. Combine eggs, sugar, coriander seeds, nuts, shortening, and orange-raisin mixture. Sift flour, baking powder, and soda together, and add to egg mixture, blending thoroughly. Turn into 2 5 by 9-inch bread pans lined with buttered wax paper. Bake in a moderate (350° F.) oven for approximately 45 minutes or until firm in center. *Makes about 35 slices.*

RAISIN CASSEROLE-BREAD WITH CARAWAY

The dough for this is soft enough to be stirred rather than kneaded.

- ⅔ cup hot water
- ⅓ cup sugar
- ¼ cup soft butter
- 2 teaspoons salt
- 2 packages (¼ ounce each) dry yeast
- ½ cup warm water
- 2 eggs, well beaten
- 1 cup raisins
- Flour for dusting
- 3 cups sifted white flour
- ¼ cup caraway seeds

In a large warm mixing bowl, combine hot water, sugar, butter, and salt. Let mixture cool to lukewarm. Dissolve yeast in the ½ cup warm water. Add with eggs to first mixture. Dust raisins with flour. Add raisins, additional sifted flour, and caraway seeds to dough. Stir briskly until well blended—about 5 minutes. Cover bowl with a warm towel and set in a warm place to rise until double in bulk, about 1 hour. Stir dough down, beating for about 1 minute. Turn into a 2-quart buttered casserole 1½ inches deep. Let rise for 20 minutes. Bake in a preheated 400° F. oven for about 45 minutes. Let cool, turn out, and cut. *Makes 12 to 15 large slices.*

CARAWAY APPLE MUFFINS

- ¼ cup butter
- ⅓ cup sugar
- 1 egg
- 2½ cups cake flour
- ½ teaspoon salt
- 4 teaspoons baking powder
- 1 cup milk
- 1 cup peeled, finely diced apple
- ½ teaspoon freshly grated nutmeg
- 1 teaspoon cinnamon
- 2 teaspoons caraway seeds
- ¼ cup sugar
- Extra butter
- 1 cup apple or rose-geranium jelly

Cream butter with sugar. Add the egg. Sift together flour, salt, and baking powder. Add to butter mixture with milk and the diced apple. Fill greased muffin cups two thirds full; sprinkle with the nutmeg, cinnamon, caraway seeds, and sugar that have been mixed together. Bake in a preheated 400° F. oven for 30 minutes, or until brown and done. Cook to lukewarm. Then, just before serving, split, butter, and spread about 1 teaspoon jelly in each muffin. *Makes about 20 muffins.*

CHOCOLATE SEED COOKIES

1 cup butter
2 cups brown sugar (packed)
2 eggs, lightly beaten
1 teaspoon vanilla
¾ cup milk
¼ cup rum
3 cups flour
2 teaspoons baking soda
¾ teaspoon salt
5 squares unsweetened chocolate
2 tablespoons butter
1 3-ounce package almonds, chopped
1 8-ounce can chopped walnuts
¼ cup sesame seeds
¼ cup coriander seeds
Chocolate shot

Cream butter and sugar until light. Add eggs with vanilla. Combine milk and rum. Sift flour with baking soda and salt, and sift again. Combine flour and milk mixtures. Mix all together. Melt chocolate with butter in double boiler. Cool. Stir in nuts and seeds and beat all together. Drop by the teaspoon onto a greased cookie sheet. Bake in a moderate (350° F.) preheated oven for 10 to 15 minutes. Frost with rum-flavored confectioners' sugar and sprinkle with chocolate shot. *Makes about 5 dozen small cookies.*

MINTED FRUIT DESSERT

1 cup grapefruit sections
1 cup orange slices
2 cups pineapple chunks
2 bananas, sliced
Juice of 1 lemon
1 cup sugar
1 cup white rum
¼ cup mixed orange mint and spearmint leaves, or candied mint leaves

Combine fruits and arrange in 6 large sherbet or champagne glasses. Blend lemon juice, sugar, and rum, and spoon mixture over fruit. Refrigerate overnight or for about 12 hours. To serve, garnish with fresh mint or candied mint leaves. *Serves 6.*

ROSE-GERANIUM CAKE

A beautiful Valentine dessert, and the Geranium Society enjoyed this too.

1 8-inch angel cake
Juice and grated rind of 2 lemons
2 cups confectioners' sugar
½ cup finely chopped rose-geranium leaves
Whole rose-geranium leaves
1 quart lemon sherbet

Split angel cake across to make 4 layers. Blend lemon juice and rind with sugar and chopped leaves. Spread half this mixture on one layer of cake, cover with second layer. Over this, spread half the sherbet. Cover with third cake layer and spread this with remaining sugar mixture. Slip into 2-quart mold and fill the center with the rest of the sherbet. Store in freezer. To serve: Unmold by loosening with a hot knife. Decorate with the whole rose-geranium leaves. Cut at once. *Serves 12 to 15.*

VALENTINE CRANBERRY CAKE

Make this the day before the party; it will cut better. For a festive appearance, frost the cake with pink icing, decorate with candied rose petals, mint leaves, and flowers—Johnny-jump-ups if they are available.

½ cup butter
¾ cup sugar
½ teaspoon salt
2 cups flour
2 teaspoons baking powder
¼ teaspoon grated nutmeg
2 cardamom seeds, crushed
2 teaspoons coriander
1 cup chopped walnuts
2 cups cranberries, chopped
½ cup currants
¼ cup sherry
¼ cup orange marmalade
5 egg whites, beaten stiff

Cream butter, sugar, and salt. Sift flour, baking powder, and nutmeg and blend with creamed mixture. Mix together cardamom seeds, coriander, walnuts, and cranberries. Add currants with sherry and marmalade. Blend into batter. Fold in egg whites. Turn into a 9 by 5-inch bread pan lined with wax paper. Bake in a preheated 325° F. oven for 2½ hours. Set pan on a cake rack to cool. *Serves 12 to 15.*

Index

About the Author

Adelma Grenier Simmons declares that "herbs are my life." At the fifty-acre Caprilands Herb Farm she revels in them—indoors, outdoors, in a shed, in a greenhouse, suspended from the ceiling, in boxes on the floor—all so beautiful and attractive with their individual aromatic odors. A natural cook, she does more than cook; in her great old-fashioned farmhouse kitchen she creates. A meal at Caprilands is forever memorable.

From April to December there is open house at Caprilands;

Mrs. Simmons lectures about herbs, and visitors tour the gardens that illustrate their history and use. Guests also sample her excellent cooking. The revival of European festivals is presently a most interesting Caprilands project.

Each year Mrs. Simmons gives many lectures through the eastern states, and she has been concerned with designing and planting various historic herb gardens in New England such as those at the Nathan Hale Homestead in Coventry, the Webb House in Wethersfield, and Mystic Seaport, all in Connecticut; and the Mission House in Stockbridge and Storranton in Springfield, both in Massachusetts.